The Myth of the Wrong Body

For Laura

unbeatable companion in the fight against my self-censorship,
who unknowingly lit the spark for this book
and continues to fuel my conquests.

For Blanca

my other part in some part,
who dared to defy the gender that oppresses us.

For Andreu and Carmen

my mentors in this craft,
for your willingness to read, write, and debate,
think and love.

The Myth of the Wrong Body

MIQUEL MISSÉ

Translated from Spanish by Frances Riddle

polity

Originally published in Spanish as *A la* conquista *del cuerpo equivocado*, 2018. Editorial Egales, S.L., Spain. © MIQUEL MISSÉ

This English edition © Polity Press, 2022

2

Support for the translation of this book was provided by Acción Cultural Española, AC/E.

AC/E
ACCIÓN CULTURAL
ESPAÑOLA

Polity Press
65 Bridge Street
Cambridge CB2 1UR, UK

Polity Press
101 Station Landing
Suite 300
Medford, MA 02155, USA

ISBN-13: 978-1-5095-5187-3
ISBN-13: 978-1-5095-5188-0 (paperback)

A catalogue record for this book is available from the British Library.

Library of Congress Control Number: 2022930008

Typeset in 11 on 14pt Warnock Pro
by Cheshire Typesetting Ltd, Cuddington, Cheshire
Printed and bound in the UK by CPI Group (UK) Ltd, Croydon

The publisher has used its best endeavors to ensure that the URLs for external websites referred to in this book are correct and active at the time of going to press. However, the publisher has no responsibility for the websites and can make no guarantee that a site will remain live or that the content is or will remain appropriate.

Every effort has been made to trace all copyright holders, but if any have been overlooked the publisher will be pleased to include any necessary credits in any subsequent reprint or edition.

For further information on Polity, visit our website: politybooks.com

Contents

Acknowledgments

This book drove me mad for a year but, luckily, I was able to count on the best possible support team on this adventure. First of all, I want to thank my amazing publisher, Egales, who are standing strong during the storm that the Spanish publishing industry is experiencing and who persist in their belief that we should keep reading a plurality of voices and ideas on the issues of gender and sexuality in Spanish. Thank you so much for opening your door to me once again with your unfailing smiles. Secondly, I want to thank the people who have sat down, pen in hand, to read and reread my drafts with patience, love, and care: Gerard Coll-Planas, Cristina Garaizabal, Laura Macaya, and Blanca Missé. Your task was not an easy one and, despite this fact, you told me what you honestly felt. I especially want to thank Gerard for his enormous generosity, for inspiring me with his discipline, his critical thinking skills, and his enormous sense of humor but, most of all, for challenging me when he disagreed. I also want to thank the people who inspired this book, the people who gave life to the initiatives of Cultura Trans and who filled the Friday evenings of Espai Trans and the Transfamilia group with their stories of resistance. I especially want to thank Pol Galofre for all the adventures we've shared: he has been the best possible partner in crafting ambitious plans with practically zero resources, almost always in over our heads but never losing the blind faith that we have to share all trans narratives no matter how minoritarian they may be. Thanks to Gracia Camps and Judit Fuster for their creativity and perseverance in the Trans Art Cabaret, our most daring attempt to promote a critical trans culture. I can't forget the team of artists who have created a shining jewel of trans culture, the creators and performers of the LIMBO show. What you've done has been very, very important for our audience, for me in particular. I also want to give thanks to my colleagues in the OASIS project, without a doubt the most passionate professional initiative I've encountered up to now: Alba Badia, Edurne Jiménez, Sara Barrientos, Silvia Merino, and Abel Huete, a brave and sensitive team with whom I've shared experiences and debates until very late into the night on how to best empower and improve the self-esteem of trans teens. And, lastly, I want to give a more personal thank you to those who have followed my process of writing this book very closely and helped ensure that I didn't get lost along the way: to Gerard, Ramon, Cris, and Empar, my unbeatable team; to Marina, for trusting me despite the distance; to Paloma, for taking the best care of me; to my small family, Carmen, Andreu, and Blanca, for being the infinite roots I always return to like a talisman. And, of course, Laura, who has taught me most of the things that I talk about in this book.

Prologue

I have the strangest feeling that my body has been stolen from me. In fact, I have the sensation that trans people in general have been robbed. It's an impression I have; I don't claim that it is the truth. But it is an intense and violent sensation, which has motivated me to write this book. I'm referring to the fact that we've been stripped of any possibility of experiencing our bodies another way. One single interpretation of some parts of our bodies has been imposed on us. As a way to explain our suffering, we've been told that we were born in the wrong bodies, but that we can make them more appropriate through hormonal treatments and certain surgical interventions. I've often felt that my body has been ravaged and for some time now I've also felt that I wanted to recover what I could of it, if there was still time. That body I hated so much, I'd now like to *reconquer*. I'd like to embrace it and apologize for abandoning it. The verb "to conquer," according to the Macmillan English dictionary, means: "to take control of land or people using soldiers." But there are more nuanced meanings that the dictionary includes if, as is always the case, you read to the end. I use the word *conquer* in italics because I want to specify that I'm referring to a conquest in the sense of "earning the love or respect of someone" (definition 4), and "gaining control of a situation or emotion by making a great physical or mental effort" (definition 2) but by no means through violence. Writing this book forms part of an almost therapeutic process of recovering my body, *reconquering* it through love, and it is also part of the political process of denouncing this uncomfortable sensation of having been robbed. But, above all, writing this book is my way of connecting with other persons who have also felt, or are feeling, that they have had something taken from them. Of course, the symbolic violence exerted on bodies in our society does not only impact trans people, so I hope this book may also serve as a bridge to dialogue with other people who, although they are not trans, have also felt or feel that they are being robbed.

I recognize that describing what I feel as having had my body stolen could be considered a problematic metaphor for many reasons, mainly because it can be argued that trans people voluntarily choose to modify our bodies. No one forces us to do it (quite the opposite; we've fought for many decades for the right to do so). This is true, but from my point of view it is also true that the conditions under which we make this decision have been and continue to be very complex. Without refuting trans people's agency and autonomy, I think it is worth careful reflection on the lack of viable alternatives to choose from when making decisions with respect to our bodies. When I started my transition I was not aware of any options besides medical treatment to modify my body, which I was told was wrong. This is why I feel like something was taken from me, like I was robbed of the possibility of experiencing my body any other way. But, as I said before, although I have personally felt that my body was wrongfully stolen, I don't claim this to be a universal truth for all trans people. It's simply something that I feel, something that pains me.

Making this accusation of robbery would be much easier if I could point out the thieves in a line-up, or exhibit evidence of their crime. But it's not that simple. I have probably been the main perpetrator in the hijacking of my body. But I am definitely not the only person responsible for the notion that there was something wrong with it. Although no one has physically run off with our bodies, the ideas we have internalized about ourselves, the discourses repeated *ad nauseam* to the point that they have infiltrated our perception of being transgender, were created by someone. What I'm trying to say is that there are persons responsible for promoting the ideas that have led us to believe the myth of the wrong body. And I think it's important to single them out.

This book aims to find the source of our notions surrounding trans bodies and to propose possible alternatives. The intention is to create a refuge. A place where we can debunk the myth that trans people have been born into the wrong body as well as the kinder, more modern fable that trans people can only live better by modifying our bodies. Right now, it often seems that the end goal of the trans movements in some parts of the world is the right to access hormonal treatments and surgical interventions in order to alter our bodies. But it is my belief that holding the right to bodily modification as the only solution to our suffering is problematic. Of course, trans people can, should, and must have this right, but centering all trans political aims on this right moves away from a question which, from my point of view, is more relevant: what actually causes the suffering that trans people feel and how can that be addressed? This question is key; the answer will determine the kinds of strategies constructed. In my opinion, this should be the central pillar of the debate on trans politics. It is also the central aim of this book: to further a constructive dialogue on how to articulate trans politics that are critical of gender normativity and, at the same time, to bring in other perspectives on the causes of the suffering felt by trans people and configure other possible solutions.

Introduction

The most popular narrative on identifying as transgender suggests that our bodies are the source of our suffering and should therefore be modified. There are other voices, however, that have tried to challenge that narrative, posing new questions: what if there is nothing wrong with our bodies? Would the solution still reside in altering the body? Finding an answer to these questions is a collective exercise that has been ongoing for decades. This book aims to participate in the effort to shift the discourse away from the myth of the wrong body. Or, said another way: these bodies of ours, which they said were wrong, can be *reconquered*.

The reflections laid out in this book are born from shared experiences in a specific historical, social, and political environment. They are framed within the Barcelona trans activism scene and its social and cultural context (Barcelonan, Catalan, and Spanish) from the early 2000s up to the publication of this book.

In the last decade, various political movements have tried to break down the notion that transgender people were born into the wrong bodies. This idea, developed by doctors in the United States around the middle of the twentieth century, gained momentum in Spain in the 1980s and 1990s after transgenderism was added to the international catalogues of mental disorders. The movement for transgender depatholo-gization emerged in Barcelona in the mid 2000s, and I count myself fortunate to have been a part of this effort, working alongside many other dedicated people to launch campaigns, organize protests, hold meetings, take trips, write manifestos, and draft communiques. In collaboration with these commit-ted trans activists (who are often not trans themselves) we've fought intense battles and, I dare say, we've achieved some small success in shifting the collective consciousness on trans issues. In my hometown of Barcelona and in many other places on the planet there are groups working toward this same goal. So, without a doubt, many people have helped lay the founda-tion for this text.

But what truly explains my need to write this book is some-thing that happened in the middle of this crusade to reframe views on the trans body. All of a sudden, trans issues became highly visible in the media, like nothing we'd ever seen before. In a matter of two or three years, we witnessed what has been dubbed the "trans revolution" by many media outlets. Our moment had arrived, trans was called to popularize, democra-tize, define itself, even "solve itself." And I, like so many other trans activists, was blown away. In shock. People reached out to say things such as "You must be so glad," "I'm happy that your movement is getting noticed," "They're finally giving you the respect you deserve," and best of all: "This is what you wanted, isn't it? Congratulations!" And I remained silent. Someone had kicked over the game board and I couldn't find any pieces to play with. An entire sector of trans activism was frozen in time on another screen, waging wars against the stigmatization and pathologization of being transgender, which seemed like something that belonged to another century in the era of the "trans revolution." Sometimes I wondered in fear if what I was feeling was rage at no longer having giants to fight, left tilting at windmills, like Don Quixote. Or maybe I was just mad that the revolution was real and we activists hadn't been the ones to stir it up. Perhaps the trans movement had been romanticized, radicalism and protest fetishized. I was bewildered, so I simply let myself be swept up in the tide. I continued to move, as if by instinct, toward the same places as always, with my now outdated battle cry against the myth of the wrong body. And at the same time I was reading all these news stories and carefully watching all these documentaries, seeing laws passed, associations emerging, and everything changing all around me.

Until I suddenly snapped out of it, and allowed myself to think critically about the avalanche of new trans references, ignoring the insistent voice in my head that said "you must be so glad." I stopped censoring my thoughts. And they led me back to the source. The myth of the wrong body was still there, it had never gone away: it had been transformed, reinvented, formally reinstated.

This books tells the story of how the myth of the wrong body that the trans person was supposedly born into has taken root in our collective consciousness, how some tried to refute it until, suddenly, a tide of "trans visibility" flooded the scene and left us stranded. Before we could speak up, articulate an opinion, we had to pull out maps and compasses to get our bearings. This story is born from the paradoxical sensation that it seems like something revolutionary is occurring in terms of trans visibility and yet there is the unshakeable sensation that this supposed revolution is tinged with profoundly conservative undertones when it comes to notions surrounding the body, gender, and identity being promoted. This book aims to dig deeper into that paradox through arguments elaborated in three parts.

In Part I, "The Source of Suffering," I will recount the conflicting narratives on the causes of suffering in trans people. The first chapter in this section, titled "Story of a Robbery," lays out the biological and medical discourses that gave rise to the myth of the wrong body and have determined the relationship between identity and the body and between gender transition and corporal modification. These discourses have been echoed by the media and public institutions and are therefore the notions that have most deeply penetrated our social consciousness, which is why we say they are hegemonic. The second chapter, "Uncovering an Alternate Narrative," considers a possible explanation of identifying as transgender that is not biological and innate. Or, said another way, it aims to dispute the biomedical narrative. Here, we will contemplate the relationship between the trans experience and social structure as well as the limits of the concepts of identity and gender expression. The third chapter, "Photo Albums, Guerrillas, Cabarets, and Other Trenches," briefly recounts my experiences as an activist with some of the trans resistance movements in Barcelona. It does not claim to be a comprehensive historical timeline of the movement but instead a kaleidoscope of sensations, debates, and self-criticisms that outline how we battled for control of the narrative and attempted to break with the classical (medical) notion of transgenderism.

Part II of the book, called "The Flood," gives a panoramic view of the initiatives that have received massive media attention and granted unprecedented visibility to trans issues in recent years. This part is made up of two chapters. The first, "Trans is Pop," is a critical analysis of the new trans role models that have emerged in North America and have had an enormous impact on Spanish society due to the influence of this culture in our social consciousness. The next chapter, "Trojan Horses in a Trans Revolution," deals specifically with the discourses surrounding being transgender in childhood in Spain.

Part III of the book, "Toward a Critical Trans Corporal Ethic," proposes a reflection on the models of empowerment that can be derived from the discourses models presented. This section consists of a first chapter entitled "Passing," a word that in trans slang refers to the ability to pass unnoticed as a trans person. Here, I will argue that trans invisibility is becoming the main currency for social acceptance, with all the problems that this implies. Finally, the last chapter, "Reconciliation," invites us to consider different forms of trans empowerment by analyzing how the social construction of our desires as well as the dominant heterosexual mindset all impact trans people's relationships to their bodies. It is also an invitation to step out of our endogamous bubble and listen to others who also live with stigmas and violence and who can provide inspiration for how to *reconquer* our bodies.

This book closes with an epilogue titled "I Remain Trapped in a Body but it's no Longer Wrong." The epilogue, which I considered making the introduction to this book, is where I'd like those readers who feel uncomfortable with my ideas to turn. I accept that, for some people, the ideas in this book will be unpleasant. In many cases they have been unpleasant for me to write, because I talk about painful experiences as well as my wishes for a different life that could have been possible for trans people if we lived in a society with different values surrounding gender and the body. Some chapters call into question notions that many trans people believe very strongly, that they may feel have saved their lives. For all these reasons, I understand that my perspective may incite pain or anger. But I hope that even trans people who feel totally opposed to my ideas will give these reflections a chance. Or, at the very least, before closing this book, please take one final minute to read the epilogue. This last section shares a personal meditation on how this political discourse can translate to everyday life and the concrete ways we can live in a manner consistent with these notions. It is an ending that I hope will temper the helplessness, defeat, and even guilt generated at times by this book's political position.

Part I

The Source of Suffering

1

Story of a Robbery

Much has been written on the origin of the myth of the wrong body (Stryker, 2017; Meyerowitz, 2004) and it is not my objective with this book to tell that story again. But, to briefly frame the concept, it can be summed up as the central notion around which the medical paradigm of transgenderism is constructed. The classic theory on why trans people exist has been constructed around the argument that trans people have a mismatch between their gender identity and their body because of an error in their biological development. The supposed natural order of things would imply that a person born in a male body would identify as a man and be masculine, and someone who is born in a female body will identify as a woman and be feminine. When this chain of events does not occur, it is understood from the medical perspective that there has been some problem of a biological nature. The mismatch is corrected by modifying the body to adapt it to the gender that the person identifies with. From there it has been instilled in the collective consciousness that a trans person is somehow trapped in the wrong body.

The predominance of the myth of the wrong body is what I presented in the prologue using the metaphor of my body having been robbed. As I said before, this robbery is not a single event but a gradual process, perpetrated by the ideas and discourses socially constructed and collectively promoted about transgenderism, even by trans people ourselves. In this chapter I will lay out what in my opinion are the four main forces driving this notion: the medical paradigm, trans people's own narratives, the market response, and our collective consciousness.

Incurable Illness, Chronic Treatment

In my house, in a folder in a file cabinet covered in dust, I keep the diagnosis that it took me five years to receive from the Gender Identity Disorders Unit (UTIG for its initials in Spanish) of the Psychiatric Department of the Barcelona Hospital Clinic. (They've now modernized and removed the word "disorder" from the Unit's name because it seemed inappropriate in these times, so now it's just referred to as the UIG.) The first thing that stands out to me when I look at it is the date (2004). It wasn't issued that long ago; it was fairly recently. I share this because many medical professionals consider the pathologization of identifying as transgender to be an outdated theoretical framework, ideas that "obviously" no one still holds. But it's not merely a theory, and it's not old, nor is it uncommon today. In fact, we still hear professionals say that they call identifying as transgender a mental disorder because the nomenclature is useful in explaining it, but that these days it doesn't have pathologizing connotations. The UIG has gradually modified its language in recent years and no longer dares to include certain terms in its diagnoses; nevertheless, the model they follow has not changed. The UIG remains blind and deaf to what for more than a decade we've been trying to challenge through trans activism. But that's an issue for another book . . . However, new initiatives have emerged within public healthcare that offer professional medical support to trans people from a truly non-pathologizing perspective, such as the Transit Clinic in Barcelona.

But let's return to the diagnosis, which is significant for several reasons. It is an acknowledgment of the suffering you've endured, recognition that something real is going on, and legitimization of the strange and painful feeling of not fitting within the system, not feeling like a woman, feeling like a man instead. You finally feel seen at a critical time when it seems like no one around you understands what is happening to you. And at the same time, it lifts responsibility from your shoulders because it is something beyond your control. It feels nice to hear that you were just born this way and it's not your fault; for someone to say that you don't have to beat yourself up anymore because there's nothing you could have done to avoid this or to make yourself feel another way. Gerard Coll-Planas digs into this issue of agency in his book *La voluntad y el deseo* [*Will and Desire*] (2010). Despite the fact that the diagnosis of an illness is often bad news, in this case it is at the same time confirmation that your suffering can be treated. This is very reassuring, especially when it comes after you've been told you have an incurable illness (if not, how devastating). Your problem can be corrected following the threefold treatment plan: psychiatric evaluation (they now use the word "psychological" because it sounds cooler), hormone treatment, and sexual reassignment surgery. In short: the suffering generated by being transgender is cured by modifying the body.

The official response to our suffering is to modify our bodies. The diagnosis confirms that there is in fact a real problem, that our subjectivity is broken and must be repaired, fixed, cured. Probably, in the moment I received my diagnosis, after so much waiting, hoping, imagining, dreaming, etc. for so long I wouldn't have wanted to hear any other explanation beyond the famous myth of the wrong body. I couldn't stand my body and I demanded the right to modify it. The mental health professionals who treated me could have provided a thousand different explanations for my suffering, but what they told me was that if I was legitimately transgender, of course I could modify my body; that in fact I had to. And I was determined to prove that I was genuinely transgender and deserving of their diagnosis.

I had already internalized the myth of the wrong body through the notions on transgenderism that existed in our social consciousness, and then people with unquestionable authority confirmed that yes, I was in fact truly transgender. They handed me a document that literally said I had an incurable illness that had a chronic treatment option involving hormones and surgeries. At the time, the process to obtain the diagnosis seemed unnecessarily byzantine but I felt that it was worth the hassle; it was a necessary step on my only possible path. It was years later that the sensation of having been robbed began to form. I ask myself why no one told me that I could have left my body the way it was, why no one ever explained that sexuality in that body was possible. There was no violence involved, no threats were made. But I feel that I was robbed of the possibility to experience my body any other way.

When I write these lines I can't help but think of my mother, who never abandoned me during that long, hard, and sometimes terrifying process. The waiting rooms in the psychiatric wards, the meetings with exhausted professors, the desperate searches on an internet illiterate to trans issues, and even my incessant anxiety were met by her with total acceptance and comprehension. The way she supported me was a lesson I carry with me as one of my greatest treasures.

And now when I ask myself why no one explained that it was possible to experience my body any other way, I know it would make her feel sad, frustrated, or even guilty. But she couldn't have explained anything to me because she didn't know any more than I did. Faced with devastating questions such as "Mom, what happens if I'm not a man or a woman?" she had no answers. That's why, as she says, she didn't stand in my way, she just stayed by my side as we marched through the shadows. And as two novices we were initiated into the cult of the wrong body. Her merit was double because it was a very a dark time, yet, despite that fact, she never abandoned her role as mother, making me feel safe, pretending that she was certain that the end was just around the corner. But yes, my mother, along with everyone else around me, accepted that the solution lay in changing my body.

The medical professionals stood before us and illuminated us with the truth in the form of a diagnosis. They could have stepped to the side as my mother had, but they didn't. Maybe they didn't know what else to do either. The purpose of this book isn't to lay blame on anyone, not the doctors who have treated us and of course not the mothers who have supported us along the way. I simply want to point out that the medical discourse on the treatment of transgenderism limited us to solutions that we paid for and continue to pay for very dearly.

We Are (Not) Desert Islands

I am not oblivious to what many of you must be thinking: how could it be a robbery when trans people themselves choose to undergo operations, if you yourself wanted to do it? To compare the medical treatment of transgenderism to a robbery is certainly risky because it makes it seem as if trans people have been forced to accept these treatments when in reality we see the exact opposite: people fighting for the right to receive hormones and have surgery. It certainly doesn't seem like anyone is forcing us to do anything.

What's more, many trans people have self-mutilated or amputated organs, sometimes leading to death, because they couldn't bear the body they inhabited. Trans people have been demanding the right to modify their bodies from the moment it became a possibility. A powerful portrait of this kind of suffering can be seen in the movie *The Danish Girl*, directed by Tom Hooper. The film tells the true story of the artist Lili Elbe and her partner, another artist named Gerda Wegener, who together faced a gender transition in 1920s Denmark. The ending reveals the dangerous turns that gender transition has implied in the past, with life itself placed at risk. This movie, as well as many other biographies of trans people, shows how in many cases trans people have literally given their lives to modify their bodies. And again, it wouldn't appear that anyone was forcing them to do it.

But from my point of view, there is nothing biological or innate about this intense rejection of the body; it has nothing to do with identifying with one gender over another. What's more, for centuries the body wasn't even slightly relevant to gender transitions; it is, in fact, a modern problem. The relationship between identity and body, or, more accurately, gender identity and body, is a twentieth-century Western concept, which assumes that if a person identifies as the "opposite" gender to the one they were assigned at birth they have to change their body to match. In my previous book, *Transexualidades. Otras miradas posibles* [*Transexualities. Other Possible Perspectives*] (Missé, 2013), I attempt to explain how the medical discourse on those who identify as transgender has a very powerful impact on the subjectivity of trans people, to the point that it can influence our internal narratives of our life stories and our relationships to our own bodies.

But if it's not something innate, how then do we explain the suffering that many trans people feel with respect to their bodies? My opinion is that the problem lies in the fact that we've been socialized in a context that naturalizes each body's assigned gender identity. Men can only have one type of body and women another. These ideas are strongly imprinted onto our self-perceptions, leading us to feel rejection toward our own bodies, specifically their sexual characteristics, when we don't identify with the gender that supposedly corresponds to us. And these social pressures are what lead us to reject our bodies, because it has been established that said body is not valid as is to house the gender we identify with. This notion that trans people's disconnect with their bodies is created by social pressures is a very unpopular argument within the trans community.

So let's break it down.

To start, the fact that social pressures affect our views of our own bodies is something experienced not only by trans people. In our everyday lives, almost all of us make decisions based on these pressures, often, if not constantly, and we don't have any problem admitting it. For example, hair removal: many women readily admit that they shave or wax because there is stigma surrounding body hair on a woman, so they feel more comfortable without that unwanted hair, even though they know that this is a learned and culturally determined beauty standard. So, although the heroic thing would be to resist these pressures, the majority of women accept the contradiction and just shave their legs. Nevertheless, it is not common to hear women say that they shave because they feel an innate rejection of their body hair. So, why is it so unpopular, especially among trans people, to suggest that our need to change our bodies is affected by a host of cultural norms surrounding gender, identity, and the body? Why is it so controversial to say that trans people modify their bodies as a consequence of these social pressures surrounding the body and identity?

I would say that there are two answers to these questions. The first is that challenging the myth of the wrong body means proposing another view of transgenderism that situates the problem in the culture and not in the body, which implies changing the culture before changing the body. And, as occurs in any process of social transformation, there are multiple actors with interest in maintaining the status quo who will demonize any discourse that could put their position at risk.

All social movements that take on unequal, unjust, or repressive systems will see pushback from the structures and persons that profit from said systems. And these institutions, when they feel their position is being jeopardized, will often work to stigmatize the movements that challenge them in order to make them invisible or even eradicate them. We don't have to look too far to see for example the constant denigration and misrepresentation of feminism, which has been ongoing for decades. These anti-feminist discourses have even filtered down into the minds of women, the very people who stand to benefit most from the feminist criticism of the patriarchy. It seems contradictory that so many women should be wary of the feminist movement but I think this occurs, among other reasons, because our patriarchal social system has stigmatized the movement and feminism hasn't had a loud enough voice to make its arguments heard (at least until very recently). If we translate this logic to the trans community and the myth of the wrong body, it is clear that hegemonic discourses define transgenderism as a condition of birth and insist that social pressures have nothing to do with it. Instead of admitting any flaw in our social structure, these actors try at all costs to individualize the problem. Said another way, the suffering felt by trans people is said to be not the result of the society they live in, but an individual problem, specific to trans people, that they can only solve by modifying their bodies, period. And critical trans activism has had its arguments drowned out or silenced, basically because what we are proposing goes against the interests of a sexist social system.

And how have the hegemonic discourses managed to shift all blame away from society where the suffering of trans people in their bodies is concerned? I would say that one of the reasons has to do with what we experience in societies that deny the importance of the group and the community in relation to individual self-esteem. Extremely individualist societies consider letting yourself be affected by society as a sacrilege.

We applaud people who won't let themselves be influenced by others, who follow their instincts, desires, and intuition, without heeding trends or social norms. People who give in to societal pressures, on the other hand, are considered dumb, basic, or lacking in personality.

You don't have to be a sociologist to come up with a criticism of this idea, pointing to the fact that human beings, as social creatures, are absolutely vulnerable to social pressures. So many things, from our self-esteem, our social relationships, and even our likelihood of being hired in the labor market, depend on our ability to meet the multiple social mandates that determine what is acceptable. I am not saying that I think these social pressures are positive; they are often unjust and aggressively exclusive to those who do not meet the standard. And small revolutions have occurred when people have dared to take a risk and question the status quo. What I am saying is that it is frowned upon in our society to admit that social pressures condition us, that what other people think affects us, that we might not be as original as we imagine. What is certain is that we are not only vulnerable to these social pressures, we are built on them. Societal norms don't only limit us, they also make us understandable to others, they construct us, they give us meaning. That is to say, our subjectivity is only possible within this framework of codes and social relationships. To be a man or woman is only possible within a social system that organizes individuals based on their biology. It is not a natural truth. And maybe we can't change that as social beings we will invent codes and categories to give ourselves meaning, but what we can and should do is challenge all forms of violence against those who fall outside social normativity by reminding ourselves that these norms and social pressures are not natural, they are not the result of any universal truth or hard fact.

But what does all this talk of social pressures have to do with trans people and their bodies? Well, a lot actually. It is common to hear trans people say that they "haven't chosen" to modify their bodies, that it's an inborn desire that can't be resisted. That they didn't undergo surgery because it's frowned upon to inhabit a trans body, but because it's something they've always wanted to do. One cliché metaphor is that if a trans person had been born on a desert island they'd still want to have surgery regardless. To sum it up, the argument implies that the desire to have surgery is something that comes before society and culture, as if that meant it was a more important desire. And I ask myself: why is a need considered more important if it's innate?

It would appear that the needs we have as human beings can be organized hierarchically: innate needs are more important than the needs that emerge because of societal pressures, which are somehow less legitimate, more frivolous, something to be overcome with a little bit of effort. Saying that the need to have surgery arises as a result of the culture, remits, in our collective consciousness, to the notion that it is a choice that a person makes because they want to. Unlike the innate, which we have no agency over, given that it's something biological that we didn't choose, culture is created by human beings, something we do have agency over. But it gets tricky: just because there is some agency doesn't mean that the social pressures we have internalized don't limit our decision making. To bring it back to our concrete example: even if the trans experience of feeling they don't belong in their bodies is caused by social pressures (and not biology) that does not mean that this feeling of not belonging can be overcome with effort. That's a very simplistic and voluntarist interpretation of how social constructs work. It's a problematic interpretation that multiple postmodern social theories have also contributed to (Coll-Planas, 2012). When we say something is socially constructed, that doesn't mean that it can simply be deconstructed, like some origami figure that can be unfolded back into a flat piece of paper, or a Rubik's cube, that can be solved with some time and intellectual effort! Frankly, in the field of social sciences, we have a whole lot of work to do in terms of explaining what it means and doesn't mean for something to be socially constructed.

And now, a third reflection: even if the desire to modify the body could be reconfigured, and if trans people were able to truly, freely choose something else and they still choose to modify their bodies, how would that be understood? It would probably be seen as a gratuitous and unnecessary modification. In fact, before the medical discourse on transgenderism had penetrated mainstream Spanish society, cross-dressing was considered a vice or a whim. But why do chosen desires have less value than those that are presented as innate?

In this same line, the researchers Coll-Planas, Alfama, and Cruells published in 2013 a very interesting study on the relationship between reconstructive surgery and aesthetic surgery.[1] In the study they compared three situations in which female breasts were constructed for different reasons: reconstruction after breast cancer, mammoplasty for trans women, and breast augmentation for cis women. (The word "cis" is used to reference persons who are not trans, that is to say, who identify with the gender identity that was assigned to them at birth.) The study showed that societal norms around gender and the body confer different degrees of legitimacy to each kind of surgery, and the perception of whether the patient should be allowed to access free medical coverage varied depending on the case.

The fact that the choices we make in our lives are only respected if we were born with a need to make them speaks to the extreme oppressiveness of our society. If our needs could all be considered equally legitimate, whatever their origin, be

---

[1] "Se_nos gener@ mujeres. La construcción discursiva del pecho femenino en el ámbito médico." [We Are Generated Women. The Discourse on Construction of Feminine Breasts in the Medical Context.]

it biological or caused by social pressures, would trans people need to hold so tightly to that fable about the desert island?

In my opinion, trans people born on a desert island wouldn't be trans: our gender expression would not be associated with any fixed gender identity and less still to a concrete social corporality. If we'd been born on desert islands we'd never dream of operating on ourselves. However, even if the desire to have an operation isn't something we're born with, it is still, for me, just as legitimate as if it were innate. The problem is that this elaborate façade we've constructed, as well as the vehement insistence of trans people that their bodies were wrong from birth, makes it even more challenging to denounce the ways in which certain social discourses have caused us to feel disconnected from our bodies.

It's like we're being assaulted by all these ideas and yet we exonerate the thieves, shouting "No one has stolen my body, I abandoned it of my own free will because it was never mine!" But yes, it was yours. It was and is the only body you have. (And I'm proposing a rescue mission!)

Market Niche

The popularization of surgery for trans people around the middle of the twentieth century opened up a totally different way of thinking about gender transition. The development of these technologies forged the path for new trans subjectivities. It's not that these treatments invented necessities that did not previously exist, but they provided a very concrete solution to the suffering experienced by trans people. Before the emergence of these technologies there were people who lived with gender identities different to the ones that had been assigned to them, but their suffering did not receive a medical response; it was managed in other ways. Their discomfort with certain parts of their bodies was accepted, although with pain and frustration. I want to be clear that the discomfort with the body experienced by trans people is not something that was invented by medical professionals. But they did invent the response to that discomfort: transform the body. Seeing the role (a starring role) that these treatments play for trans people today, it is clear that the medical discourse has won the cultural battle to control the narrative on the origin of trans suffering: the myth of the wrong body. But the problem is not the technology, rather who and what it serves.

In Spain, sexual reassignment surgeries were de-penalized in 1983, when the crime of lesions was eliminated from the Penal Code. Until then these types of modifications to the body had been considered illegal forms of castration. In the late 1980s, Spanish surgeons began traveling to other countries to train and brought these surgical techniques back home. In the years that followed, this small circle of surgeons began operating and hundreds of trans people in Spain underwent surgeries. It goes without saying that prices for these treatments increased astronomically and the results weren't that great at first but they have evolved and improved over the years as many trans bodies have served as training grounds.

Starting in 2008, medical treatments for trans people, among them surgical interventions, were included in the catalogue of treatment options offered by the public health system in all of Spain, except Andalucía, which had already incorporated them way back in 1999. Today, each region designates a medical unit to take charge of these treatments (the so-called Gender Identity Disorder Units, now Gender Identity Units). The Units decide how many surgical interventions can be carried out by the public system each year, and trans people anxiously wait for their names to inch to the top of the long wait lists. Those who tire of waiting turn to the private market. That is to say, surgeons in private clinics are still in great demand to the point that it is uncommon to meet someone who had their surgery in a public hospital.

The official version of events ends here, but I think it's worth mentioning the role these medical professionals have played in this story.

Let's return to diagnosis. Starting in the late 1980s, the health professionals who worked with trans people touted the famous threefold treatment method (psychological or psychiatric evaluation, hormonal treatment, and surgery). They doled out diagnoses explaining to people that they had "an incurable illness, with chronic treatment options," which consisted of hormonal therapy and surgery. And these treatments were not publicly funded until almost twenty-five years later. The results: trans people became a succulent market niche. (They tell us that we have the wrong body and then we pay them . . . It has to be admitted that this is a brilliant business model.)

Among the surgeons most recognized in Spain in the field of so-called "gender reassignment surgery" a few figures stand out in terms of how they've built their practice on the myth of the wrong body. These are professionals with dubious reputations: surgeons who have been working for decades and have treated thousands of trans people, and whose businesses are booming, despite their horrible reputations among the trans community. In my experience as an activist I've heard many terrible stories of very questionable results sold as infallible cures, claims from people who wanted to report malpractice but were not able to because before they entered the operating room they'd signed multiple documents that impeded them from later filing complaints, many tales of trans people referred to using their original gender pronouns on the operating table.

And, as the icing on the cake, some of these doctors are the main referents for our mass media. It seems there's not a panel discussion, debate, TV news report, or documentary on being transgender that they're not a part of. There they are in their offices, sitting in front of their computers and behind the screensaver pictures of our bodies before and after we lie down on their table. But the best is what they're saying: that the problem with people who have gender identity disorder is that they were born in the wrong body blah blah blah . . . Chameleon-like media figures who, a decade ago, talked about us as though we were sick but who quickly learned that that's fallen out of fashion.

But wait, there's more. We could ask ourselves how these professionals have managed to become experts in this field. Well, in some cases they formed part of the medical teams of the Gender Identity Units. Consultations in which they told people that in order to be cured they had to have an operation but, unfortunately, the treatment wouldn't be covered by the public health system. And then they tell them that there's a place they might be able to go . . .

Guess which place? To these surgeons' private clinics. But wait, aren't they the same doctors who worked in the public hospital medical units? Bingo! They refer patients to themselves. And that's how it went for many years.

Some of these medical professionals have taken other, even more slippery paths. They've learned how to monetize trans people's need for sexual reassignment, mainly women, by creating an extensive catalogue of bodily modifications that go very, very far beyond what could be considered any form of treatment. To prove this, a colleague of mine went to one of these clinics explaining that she was a trans woman who wanted to have a vaginoplasty. She walked out with a 70,000 euro estimate for the procedure. The doctor had added on to the vaginal reconstruction multiple retouches for "feminization" of her face and body. If you want to be a woman you will need a pinch of this, a splash of that, and a large dollop of that over there. The websites for these clinics show that the catalogue of treatments for trans women is significantly more extensive than for trans men. Would that have anything to do with the fact that we live in a sexist society that is constantly imposing impossible demands on women's bodies? In this sense trans women are a much more interesting business prospect than cis women (women who are not trans) because to the former we've said that corporal modification is the chronic treatment for our incurable illness and to the latter we've said they are frivolous. It is easy to become trapped by the myth of the wrong body because it doesn't specify when treatment will end, and the reality is that treatment never ends, neither trans people nor anyone else can ever have a perfectly male or perfectly female body because that body does not exist. If you don't believe it, you must never have seen a tabloid shot of a starlet's cellulite at the beach. We are not only a market niche, we are also a limitless market, a black hole, a bottomless well.

The first time I visited the website of one of these doctors, who was a lion of trans marketing, I was welcomed with a message I still haven't recovered from. It said "Beauty is on the inside." Is this guy a genius or what? The message is no longer there, they eventually took it down and my blood pressure thanks them. What hasn't changed is the web address, the name of the project, which is also priceless: cirugiadegenero .com [gendersurgery.com]. It can't be said more clearly: these are operations that have to do with gender, with culture, with how our society sees men and women's bodies. Now, what will really make you fall out of your seat are the tabs that lead to the catalog of surgeries for trans men: "female transgender" and for trans women: "male transgender."

The first chapter of the non-existent book *Basic Rules for Dealing with Trans People* would read: "Trans women should be addressed in the feminine." Some people have no shame.

But let's move on. This specific website is targeted toward trans people but, if we go to the clinic's main site, we see that these surgeries are only some of the many options available. There are other offerings directed mainly toward cis women, with a specific section on genital surgeries. It's funny to me that, in this sea of options, gender surgery is only something for trans people: the treatments offered to cis women are simply called plastic surgery or female genital surgery. It's surprising to me because these are all gender surgeries.

Some of these doctors have undeniably benefitted from the myth of the wrong body. They've prospered economically, bathed their public persona in an aura of progressivism and courage for having treated trans people, and they have invented new surgeries that at the same time generate new needs in people.

It is truly shocking that I was taught to hate some parts of my body while there are people who literally make a living from that hate, who get rich modifying our bodies. And although, of course, there are some well-meaning professionals, the end result is the same.

2

Uncovering an Alternate Narrative

For a long time, critical trans activism has preferred not to question the origin of transgenderism, maintaining that what is truly relevant were the roots of transphobia instead. Although I understand this idea, in recent years I've realized that to combat the monster of gender essentialism it's not enough to ignore it. We also need a counter discourse that proposes another paradigm.

The fight for the depathologization of those who identify as transgender has followed this same logic: we fiercely defend the notion that what trans people experience is not an illness but without putting forward any other theory to explain it. But trans activism's refusal to enter into debate about the biological origins of transgenderism, and therefore gender, has proven fairly inefficient. As we will see later, biologically centered discourses have not only not disappeared, but have even adapted to the context; they have evolved and strengthened.

That's why I think that the time has come to change our position and enter into the fray with our arguments, fully aware that the hegemony of the biomedical/scientific discourses put us at a disadvantage. Formulating a critical response to the origin of transgenderism is important not only as counterargument to the classical discourse but also something our own trans community needs. We need to be able to talk about ourselves beyond purely oppositional discourses, we need a position that is not simply that we don't agree with the official discourse. We need to get our hands dirty and express our point of view so that people can decide what to do with it, if it serves them, to see if it's a good fit for them or not. And, at the same time, the process will be profoundly revelatory in terms of exposing where our supposed trans allies stand, whether or not they are truly allies or, to the contrary, if they uphold gender and identity paradigms that we don't share.

This chapter aims to uncover an alternate narrative on the possible origin of transgenderism based in post-structuralist theories that are critical of the classical conception of the subject. It doesn't claim to be a truth, but merely one subjective interpretation, which will surely have some blind spots or leave some questions unanswered. But the truly relevant question is whether it serves us collectively to begin to think about the interpretative framework surrounding the trans experience. This interpretation is up for debate.

The Gender Identity Problem

Transgender and trans experiences in general became an object of study in medicine in the early twentieth century in Europe, but the emergence of these theories first occurred in the United States in the 1950s. These discourses, which have had multiple ramifications, were founded in the notion that human beings go through a natural process of identity development. Although it was pointed out in the first chapter, it's worth revisiting the symbolic sequence of events that this implies: when a person is born in a male body they should identify as a boy, then a man, and when a person is born in a female body they should identify as a girl and later as a woman. This is what is supposed to occur naturally; when this does not happen it means there is some problem in the brain that interrupts the proper development of gender identity. This is why some theories posited that being transgender was a mental disorder, others claimed it was a form of intersexuality in the brain, others believed that the cause was a hormonal defect. But they all had something in common: if a person is transgender it's because something developed incorrectly in their body.

To challenge these notions, the discourses centered on depathologization of those who identify as transgender have argued that being transgender is not an illness and that to call it one is stigmatizing. They explained that transgenderism as a form of existence is just as natural as any other and that there is nothing pathological about it. But what the depathologizing discourses have not done is take the time to pick apart what it concretely means to be "a form of existence just as natural as any other," they have not explained what the relationship is between being born in a body with certain sexual characteristics and identifying with a certain gender.

The question I feel we need to be asking isn't what makes a person NOT identify with the gender that corresponds to their biological sex, but what makes a person identify with any one gender over another, no matter what kind of body they are born in. Or, to put it another way, our questioning should center on why people born with male characteristics feel that they are men. The biomedical discourse on identifying as transgender claims that what is natural and correct is for a person born in a male body to identify as a boy, then a man. And it is precisely here that we find the underlying problem. What is natural about someone identifying with one of these categories simply for having been born in a certain body?

Estrangement

To answer this question I propose that we put on our researcher hats and practice the technique of estrangement. Estrangement is a method of social research that consists of observing the most mundane situations and trying to analyze them as if they were totally novel. The idea is to become estranged from something that feels ordinary in order to pick apart how much of it is culturally learned, customary, and traditional. If we moved to a part of the world with cultural codes completely different to our own, estrangement would occur automatically because we would naturally be puzzled by what we saw. Many of what the people there considered mundane situations would be surprising or inexplicable to us. The challenge lies in performing the inverse of this exercise. It is hard to imagine how our own daily customs would look through the eyes of someone from far away. But I propose we employ this method to examine gender identity. Let's imagine that we had to explain the concept to a Martian who doesn't know what it means, how it happens, where its origin lies.

I would venture to say that many trans people (and others as well) have experienced authentic periods of estrangement from gender identity. Also, anxiety, anguish, rage, frustration, impotence, isolation, pain, etc. . . . but let's leave it at estrangement. Gender identity is a profoundly mundane concept that we never stop to think about until it causes some problem and then suddenly it's dumped on our heads like a bucket of cold water. It's so ingrained and automatic for most people that they don't even know there is a name for this feeling, that it is called gender identity.

We'll start at the beginning. (Buckle up, Martian!) Gender identity describes the gender category that a person identifies with: in our society we have two choices: you can identify as a man or as a woman. The categories are tied to language: people who identify as men are referred to using masculine pronouns and people who identify as women are spoken of using feminine pronouns. The majority of people don't think of gender as something someone simply identifies with but something that someone *is*. There is not much awareness of what gender has to do with identification because it is widely accepted that gender is something that you are born with. You are born male or female and there's no need to think more about it. Sometimes when I've asked people if they identify as a man or a woman they've responded that they didn't understand the question, but in any case they told me that they WERE a woman or they WERE a man. In fact, the majority of times adult people answer this question by referring to their genitals, which is to say their biology, and children speak about their interests, behaviors, and gender expressions. But very few people can clearly explain what it actually feels like to be a man or a woman. And at the same time it's paradoxical because trans people are asked nonstop to explain how and why we know that we feel like men or women, a question the majority of the population has no idea how to answer. What's more, they don't have the foggiest idea that they even have a gender identity because they've never asked themselves about it. This is similar to the way many white people have no idea that they have a skin color.

If our Martian is still here and hasn't rocketed off, it would be very interesting to hear what they are thinking. I'd like to take a guess at what they might think of this strange code we call gender identity. They'd probably say that gender identity is frankly a very strange construct, vague and ambiguous to the point that it is very confusing. Here are a few of the questions a Martian might ask: how does a person know if they are a man or woman? What does it feel like to be a man or a woman? Does it feel different in each case? Can you stop being one or the other? Can you be both things at the same time? Can a person not know what their gender identity is? Does every single person even have one? Can you live without a gender identity or will you die if you don't have one? Do people feel like a man or a woman all the time, on the subway, on the street, at work and at school too, or only during some moments of the day or night? How does being born with a penis and testicles make a person feel like a man?

The Martian could go on, the questions are infinite. The problem is: do we have answers? Does anyone know the answers? Do you know the answers to any of these questions? Feeling like a man or a woman is profoundly relative, it's a specific, subjective experience and at the same time it's a socially constructed, collective experience as well. Asking the people around us about their gender identities proves a very interesting exercise. The responses, fascinating and revealing, show us that there is not one single truth.

Our Parents Are Our Gender Identity

The questions the Martian might ask do have answers, the ones provided by biology and medicine. In short, the explanation goes, when a person is born in a body with female sex characteristics their brain must somehow also be imprinted with the message that they are female and so naturally they will identify with other women and define themselves as a woman. According to the biomedical theory, gender identity itself is something that people feel because it is part of their natural essence. By the time toddlers begin to speak they already know whether they are boys or girls.

But there are some of us who want to challenge that response. We are not in agreement with what it implies, which feels dangerous to us. If we were to leave a newborn baby on a desert island, with no other humans, to be cared for by a pack of wolves, and we returned to visit after fifteen years, when we asked them if they were a boy or a girl their most likely response would be to bite us. They most likely would not feel like either a boy or a girl, they wouldn't identify with other boys or girls, they would most likely identify with wolves. There is nothing innate or biological about identifying as a boy or girl, it is learned through culture, language, and the messages we receive early on about what group we belong to. Babies are not born naturally knowing whether they are a man or woman: they learn this from society. A person born with female sex characteristics will not know that their body belongs to the social group "woman" and that this is different to the "man" group if no one tells them. That is to say, it's relational, constructed in opposition to something else. In order for someone to feel like a woman they have to know that there are men, and that men don't feel like women.

I'm not saying anything new here. The notion that gender is socially learned has been developed extensively by feminist theories and movements, as well as by constructionist traditions in social sciences. Much reflection has been given to how gender is learned in relation to a person's values, tastes, preferences, behaviors, and desires. I'm simply translating these arguments to the formation of gender identity.

Simply Put, We Lie

That gender identity is counterintuitive can be evidenced through observing the way children behave and question these categories. Many of them take a while to figure out how gender identity works. It takes them a while to learn it because the norms are often absurd, exclusive, and exclusionary. Where is it written that it has to be this way?

We don't say to children: "When you decide whether you are a boy or a girl you can let us know. You can take your time to figure out which one you identify with more. If you don't feel like either a boy or a girl that's absolutely fine. If just for today you feel more like a girl or a boy that's fine too."

What do we say to them, then? Nothing. We don't tell them anything because we take it as a given that they know what they are. So we never have a conversation about it. We leave them to their own devices. They learn what they are the hard way, and when they cross the line we explain the rules to them. When a boy declares out of nowhere: "I want to be a girl today!" an adult will speak up to explain, "No, no, Clara is a girl, you are a boy." And we leave it at that. Or the day comes, all of a sudden, when they need to go to the bathroom and they have to choose a door. They are forced to reject the other. Without having to say a word, we assume that they'll know which bathroom to go into because it should be an innate certainty. And I wonder, why do we bother to lie? I'm sure there are many children who would be thankful if, for once, an adult could recognize that the whole thing about being a boy or girl is kind of ridiculous so it's okay if they don't understand it. I'll go even further to say that telling kids there should be a natural concordance between the body, gender identity, and gender expression is a form of symbolic violence. We are injecting them with a virus that keeps them from growing and expressing themselves freely without feeling guilty about their desires.

Our Other Identities: Divorcee, Catalan, etc.

At this point, some of you may be saying that we were doing fine until we got all relativist about gender identity, that it's one thing to analyze critically the notion of being transgender and another very different thing to say that our gender is constructed by our parents. Well, I'd like to propose a thought exercise that shows how our identities are more flexible than we think. All we have to do is compare gender identity with other identity categories that have changed over time. Although right now it seems impossible to imagine a world in which being a man or woman could play an insignificant

role in a person's identity, there are other categories which
not long ago were deemed essential to our identities but are
no longer considered relevant today. Let's take as an example
marriage. For decades in our society it was very important to
know a person's marital status. It was a crucial piece of information that determined how we could interact with a person,
especially a woman. Knowing whether or not a girl was single,
married, widowed, or a nun was profoundly relevant to the
social relationship between this girl and any boy. To such an
extent that our marital status figured on our national identity
cards. The range of possible statuses was strict and definitive.
It was something that you would be for life: a nun for your
whole life, spinster forever, married until widowed, and then a
widow, without another partner, for the rest of your life. And
divorce, obviously, was something totally unimaginable. But
then after much social struggle, mainly thanks to feminism,
marital status began to lose importance as an identity category,
people's choices became more flexible, as did the possibility
to move from one marital status to another throughout the
course of a lifetime. Today it's infrequent for people to define
themselves by their civil status. When we meet someone new
it's not common to immediately ask whether they are married;
this is considered non-essential information. And that's not
to say that the concept has disappeared, that marital status
as a category is dead, that these words have disappeared from
the dictionary. What has happened is that it has become less
relevant, it has been relativized. The same words are still used
but we've freed them of such corseted meanings, and when
we use them we aren't describing an entire life or a type of
person in essence, we are simply describing a specific moment
in someone's life, their current, but not necessarily permanent
relationship status.

Let's turn now to national identity, which seems to me an
excellent example of our capacity to be flexible. People today
asking about national identity will receive many different

answers: "Well, I feel Catalan" or "I feel Catalan and Spanish." Even "I feel Catalan and Spanish and also Peruvian because even though I was born here my parents are from Peru and I feel like I'm from there too" and even "I feel Catalan, Spanish, but also Italian because I went to an Italian school and when I travel to Italy or listen to Italian music it's like going home in a way." But also "I have no idea, it doesn't matter to me. I don't identify with any national identity, I'm from my neighborhood." There are a thousand possibilities, and all of them are considered valid. We can understand them all, and we don't try to evaluate whether they are possible, authentic, or compatible with the person's biology. They are simply people's impressions of their national identity. Let's now compare this plurality with our rigidity in thinking about gender identity: that thing you have to know with certainty from childhood, that you have to feel naturally, that can only be one thing or another, that can't be neither, that can't be all of the above. It's crazy! Why can't we transfer this flexibility about marital status or nationality to the realm of gender identity?

No One Is Born Transgender

If gender identity isn't a biological fact, neither is being transgender. You are not born a man or a woman, you are born with a body that has given sex characteristics, but from there to feeling like a man or woman there is no innate relationship. So you can't be born transgender either. If anyone out there is thinking that what I'm suggesting sounds like science fiction, I'd ask them to listen to the main scientific argument used today to explain being transgender as something we're born with: apparently while we were in our mothers' wombs, a shower of hormones soaked into our bodies, but not our heads, making the body evolve into one sex and the brain into another. Which sounds more like science fiction?

Honestly, the hormone shower theory seems pretty weak to me because it implies that feeling like a man or a woman depends on neurological and hormonal factors that take place in the mother's womb, which is to say, independent of culture, regardless of society. But beyond that, the theory is unprovable: to know for sure, we'd have to study the brains of unborn infants who would have turned out to be transgender persons in adulthood and compare them to fetuses that wouldn't have identified as transgender when they grew up. It's impossible to do this because there's no way to know who is going to be transgender and who isn't. And if we study the brains of adult transgender persons and compare them to the brains of non-transgender adults, how can we know that whatever that shows us about the brain has to do with something that happened while they were gestating in their mother's womb. or if it's a product of their life experience and the environment they grew up in?

I think there are other, better explanations and I'd like to share them.

Rigidity

Let's go. Transgenderism and the trans experience in general has to do with rigidity. The categories of man and woman are so terribly rigid that they end up excluding people. It's so difficult to be a masculine man or a feminine woman that in fact many people feel they fail to meet gender norms. And I'm not only talking about trans people, but all people who live in Western societies in which gender is the central pillar of subjectivity and social relationships. Being a man has so many rules, limits, pressures, and mandates, that it's very likely a person who was assigned male at birth will feel at odds with this identity at some point in their life. Sometimes they may feel that they aren't man enough, that they are not like other men, that they aren't sufficiently masculine. And the same thing happens to women. Although it is true that feminist movements have tried to shift these norms, being a woman is still suffocating. These models are so rigid that it should worry us if people didn't feel tension with the categories of man/woman, or masculine/feminine. And if we don't feel it, it's because our indoctrination is so complete that we lose all curiosity about exploring other gender expressions: we simply obey and comply with the norms to keep from being expelled from our peer groups or because we don't even have enough breathing room to consider breaking with these norms.

Someone might misinterpret me as insinuating that people who've never felt any discomfort with their gender category have been brainwashed by the doctrine of gender norms. It's not about that. But it would surprise me to hear about someone completely enamored with being a man or woman, who has never ever felt frustrated or limited by their gender at some time in their life (for example, in childhood). Maybe they just don't remember having learned gender rigidity at two or three years old.

Feeling discomfort with gender is not a rare experience reserved for trans people; just the opposite. It is a widespread, yet seldom mentioned, unease but there is little space to express it. And what is interesting is how people deal with this discomfort: sometimes they conquer it, rejecting all things that cause them to feel unease; sometimes they try to compensate, seeking other ways to feel fulfilled; sometimes it leads to a gender transition. That is to say that the trans experience is one possible way to address a kind of discomfort that many people feel to varying degrees. We can't think about trans people in isolation, trying to understand why they've decided to transition without understanding that they make up part of a much larger group of people who feel profound discomfort with gender rigidity. The trans experience is one possible solution in the face of this discomfort but the common factor is the discomfort itself. This is what we need to focus on, the enemy to be vanquished: if we can lessen suffering, the need to transition will also be less acute. That is to say that a society in which trans people exist is not exactly my utopic ideal; when there is transgenderism it's because there is suffering; it is a symptom of the rigidness of our gender categories. Or said the other way around, my utopic ideal would be a constant state of transition, where we feel free to explore our gender expressions without limits, expectations, or punishment. The rigidity is so extreme that, often, when a person who should identify as a man does not identify with many of the classic values of masculinity and identifies more with the values of femininity, the only explanation offered is that they must truly be a woman. The real explanation is that masculinity is an absurd conglomeration of stereotypes. The category is so powerful that when we don't fully fit inside it we think that there is something wrong with us. We never stop and examine the category itself.

But, returning to the previous notion, gender transition is not the only possible route to easing this suffering. In fact, there are many people in our society who feel uncomfortable with gender rigidity and yet they don't all transition. Most of us know very feminine men, very masculine women . . . So I ask myself: are these people wrong?

I have a single sister (a very singular sister) who is two years older than me, named Blanca. In our adolescence we were, by the prevailing social standards, two very masculine girls. Today my sister is a very masculine adult woman and I'm a not-so-masculine trans man. In a way, we both occupy an intermediate space, a gray area, she as a very masculine woman and I as a not-so-masculine man. The question is: why did I have a gender transition when she didn't? Do I have a man's brain but she doesn't? Or is it that I received a shower of hormones in my mother's belly that she didn't? How do you explain our different paths? Well, basically the answer is that, in the face of a similar discomfort, each of us developed different survival skills. We were two girls up against a society that conceived of womanhood in tremendously rigid and limited ways. For me, it made sense to think that I felt the way I did because I was truly a man. She did not reach the same conclusion. And we will never know if I made the right choice or not, or if she should have transitioned too. There is no absolute truth, there are no assurances as to which of the two decisions is correct: they are two equally valid survival strategies. And the choices we make are based on many complex factors, conscious and unconscious, our beliefs, things we've learned, our self-esteem, our connections, our desires.

Just one note: because I truly felt that I was a man, I felt the need to modify my body. My sister never felt this, and I'd venture to guess that she maintained a much healthier relationship to her body than I did. I think it's because when she rejected the trans narrative, she also rejected a specific subjectivity that linked her identity to the modification of her body. (She managed to thwart the attempt to steal her body whereas I was cleaned out.)

My sister participated in the process of editing this book, and when she got to this part she suggested adding a brief explanation of her perspective on our experiences. (Thank you, Blanca, for helping me tell the story of our choices!)

I have one brother, Miquel, who says that I am "a very masculine adult woman" and he is a "not-so-masculine trans man." It's a fairly accurate characterization, but the most accurate part is what he says about us both having experienced our gender in "an intermediate space, a gray area." It's funny because people who meet us for the first time always remark how "similar" we are, and this likeness is essentially the similarly gray or ambiguous genders that we each inhabit – despite the different social genders that we each identify with.

The only true difference in gender that my brother and I have had, now more a thing of the past, was the issue of his relationship with his body, which this book so eloquently addresses, something we argued about a lot during his transition. But I certainly felt at the time that transforming his body to become more masculine had taken on existential dimensions for my brother, so I fully supported his decision.

As he says, we'll never know why my brother went through a transition and I didn't, but what I do know is that his brave, thought-out, and determined transition has freed me of uncertainties surrounding my own gender, which was still partially trapped in a repressive and normative framework – as everyone's gender is. He empowered me to experience my own masculine gender expression with more freedom, to accept myself as I am, overtly masculine, without needing to change my body. His transition has been tremendously liberating for me – although that's something I only realized several years after the fact: thank you, Miquel.

With his transition another even greater transition occurred: a kind of inversion of our sibling relationship that went beyond a "change" in gender: he became the older sibling paving the way for me. I followed along as my brave adventurer of a little brother forged a path through the dense jungle with his machete, allowing light to shine down on us all. Since he underwent his transition, I have been able to question myself more openly about whether I too wanted to step into that space of experimentation with gender expression that he generously created for both of us.

It is also true that I was able to escape those who would rob me of my body, whereas he, in a way, was stripped bare. But it's easier to see the thieves coming when you're traveling at the back of the convoy. You have time to hide. My brother couldn't escape, he had no choice but to stand and fight. And now we must stand together in the war against social classes and gender categories. Not only do we have enemy troops to face, often with grave losses, but we must also undo the social and cultural frameworks in which these enemy forces have framed the fight itself. And if we don't achieve that second and more difficult transformation we will never be free.

As a Marxist, I know that those who fight, while they may suffer and they may often lose, will be rewarded with a greater freedom (my brother won the battle to affirm his gender identity) and in their fight they will gain deeper understanding of their freedom. Although it's true that he had to suffer more alienation from his body than I did, Miquel, through his struggle and courage, achieved a greater degree of freedom than I did. So as contradictory as it might sound, the suffering, pillaging, and plundering he endured ultimately freed him to inhabit his body as his own home (once he'd recovered it, of course).

Just one note: I've told my brother that I don't like his use of the word "conquer" to talk about a stolen body that has to be reclaimed. It is precisely all the suffering he's undergone, putting his body in the line of fire and facing the physical and symbolic violence that trans bodies experience daily that allows him now to think of his body beyond instrumental, technological, and military terms. The revolution in "gender identity" that has been initiated by trans people will lead to a revolution in the ways all of us inhabit our bodies, which define us socially, to a defiance of the normative, commercialized, productive, instrumental, capitalist system. This book contributes to the reconstruction and restoration of the relationship between body and gender from the small liberated territory that all our trans brothers and sisters have won. I have faith that they are going to continue to show us the way forward, and I will continue trying to resolve, despite difficulties and losses, other urgent issues of the class struggle.

Writing a book can bring with it touching surprises such as my sister's words in the preceding paragraphs. If she hadn't contributed to this book, I'd probably never have known how she felt. (Thanks again for this beautiful gift, Blanca.)

One of the main objectives of this reflection on the trans experience is to expand thinking on trans issues to a broader context. Trans people make up a small portion of the greater population, but many more people feel discomfort with their gender to varying degrees. So, instead of focusing on trans people specifically, it might be more useful to home in on the gender norms at the root of this suffering, independently of the ways in which they are later addressed. I often notice that people think that trans people are radically different from them, different in essence, that trans people experience something that cis persons have never felt. And that idea is very problematic because it keeps people from connecting with the ideas or sensations that have led someone to initiate a gender transition. And connection with these experiences is key to being able to empathize, to being able to imagine ourselves in that position, to see that we could all just as easily be trans. I think that if trans people were able to guide others through the labyrinth of thoughts and sensations that we go through to reach the conclusion that we want to transition, many people would be able to identify with us.

Archeology of Empathy

I want to share an example that I think illustrates the idea that could be summarized as "To understand an experience you have to be able to imagine yourself in that position." For years I gave workshops in schools on gender and sexuality (my respect goes to all the workshop leaders around the world doing invisible, precarious, underappreciated but very important work in our classrooms). In that context I did some (informal) social research on the heterosexual adolescent consciousness, a fascinating world to say the least.

One of the most revelatory exercises involved a simple question. I first asked only the heterosexual girls in the class to raise their hands if they could imagine, at any point in their long lives, hypothetically, maybe, even if only in their own minds and never acting on it, could they imagine feeling desire toward another girl. The answers came quickly with the majority of girls raising their hands as they glanced around whispering to each other. "Life is long, who knows? Why not?" Right after that I'd ask the same question to the heterosexual boys. Could they imagine, at any point in their long lives, hypothetically, maybe, even if only in their own minds and never acting on it, feeling desire toward another boy? After the initial shock, the bursts of laughter, exclamations, and furtive glances, one or two hands might go up, if any. Some of the boys would shout out "Sorry, teach, but that could never happen to me!" And then I'd ask them again how they could be so sure since they had so many years left to live. The answer was always something along the lines of "I just know, that could never happen to me, not ever, it could just never happen."

Without entering into a detailed analysis of these responses, which would be enough to fill another book entirely, I'd like to point out two things. The first is that the girls, who were just as heterosexual as the boys, allowed themselves greater flexibility in imagining feeling desire toward another woman. Secondly, the boys in general had extreme difficulty with this. It had nothing to do with heterosexuality, because the girls identified as such and nevertheless they could imagine something else, but the boys could not. You don't have to be a genius to imagine that maybe one factor in the boys' answers was homophobia, a key pillar in the traditional construction of masculinity. When I asked them if they thought that their answers had anything to do with homophobia they'd furiously proclaim that this wasn't the case at all, that they had gay friends, that they had no problem with homosexuality, that they simply didn't feel any desire toward other males and would never, never ever, not even hypothetically, feel that desire to the day they died.

These kinds of responses, repeated over and over, made me think that heterosexual girls were more readily able to put themselves in the place of feeling homosexual desire. That is to say, they empathized with the lesbian desire precisely because they could imagine themselves in that situation. The boys on the other hand thought of a gay man as something they could never be, like someone fundamentally different to them. And that's precisely the problem, that they couldn't put themselves in that position. They could accept another person's homosexual desire but it was something that they were never going to experience, it didn't form part of their universe of possibilities. And I asked myself how those heterosexual boys could possibly understand and accept homosexuality, as they vehemently maintained, if it was something that they could not even imagine experiencing. And I am certain that heterosexual male acceptance of gay men occurs because they can in fact imagine this desire, an ambiguous desire, maybe homosexual at some point or maybe not. It means that they can embrace the uncertain, hypothetical possibility of feeling that desire.

This example helps me explain the idea that in order to understand or accept another person's homosexual desire you have to be able to connect with this desire within yourself. Heterosexuality, homosexuality, bisexuality, and the entire range of possible sexual orientations are not intrinsic traits. They are sexual preferences that are in large part constructed socially. And with trans people, I'd say the same thing happens. In order to truly embrace the notion of trans, you have to be able to see yourself in that place, even just for a second, to be able to imagine that moment when a person questions their identity, when they feel a pang of doubt over our gender categories. You have to be able to let yourself fathom that uncertainty surrounding gender identities, even if it makes you feel vulnerable and uncomfortable. You have to be able to conceive of the notion that we are all very close to being trans, that it's not an experience far removed from your own, just the opposite. We are all just one millimeter away from being trans, just as, pointed out by Fausto-Sterling, we are all one millimeter away from being considered intersex by the rulers that measure our genitals at birth, since one millimeter difference is enough to place a person in one category over another, a single millimeter (Fausto-Sterling, 2006).

We Are Truman

In my mind, gender is something like in the movie *The Truman Show*. (If you haven't seen it, jump to the next section because this is a total spoiler.) Truman is a happy guy with a perfect life. Everything is going smoothly in all areas, excellently, in fact. At work, at home, in his community, everything, everywhere is perfect. But one day Truman gets curious . . . huge mistake! He has the urge to leave his perfect town, his perfect job, his perfect family. He wants to travel, explore the world, which he's never seen before. So he sets to work: he tries to take off in his car, but all the roads are closed, he tries to buy a plane ticket, but none of the travel agencies has any flights available, he tries to get away by boat, but huge storms keep him from sailing away. There's no way to get out of his town. But he's persistent, he takes the boat out again and, despite the huge waves, he manages to reach the open ocean, nothing but blue horizon and empty sea all around. And, just when he's managed to escape that perfect world, the boat suddenly stops: he's hit something. It's the sky, which is, in reality, a wall painted to look like the sky, a stage setting. It's all a set. Truman has unknowingly lived his entire life on a television soundstage, starring in a program that had been broadcasting his life, live, from the moment he was born. That's why he was never able to escape his perfect, happy life. And it seems to me that in a way we're all Truman and the soundstage is like our world, so rigid when it comes to gender, where we're supposed to be happy, to fit in, and when we try to explore other things we realize there's no escaping. We all live on a soundstage like Truman but it only becomes evident when we try to sail out into the open ocean; only then do we discover the wall painted to look like sky. Just because you've never hit that wall doesn't mean that the wall doesn't exist and that your personal experience with gender isn't also profoundly rigid, limited, and even sometimes painful. I crashed against that wall and now I can't stop thinking about it. I sit on the dock, staring at it, analyzing it, preparing to challenge it, to resist it.

As I was saying, the limits surrounding the body, gender, and identity imposed by social norms don't only affect trans people. To give a few examples, cis women can alter their breast size without too much trouble at any private plastic surgery clinic in Barcelona, but they can't have their breasts removed without a diagnosis of gender identity disorder within the context of a transition. A cis woman can freely feminize her body (to the extent she can afford it) but she can't as readily get rid of or surgically remove the parts of her body considered feminine. The majority of cis women don't even notice this limit because they don't seek out mastectomies, but if they did, they'd run up against Truman's wall. This injustice is something that the members of the group "Marimachos Cancerosas" [Dykes with Cancer] set out to expose. One of their activists developed cancer and had to have one of her breasts removed. When the moment for her reconstructive surgery arrived, she asked that in place of reconstructing the breast that had been removed, they simply remove the other one too. The response was an emphatic no. After many months of fighting she managed to get the surgery she wanted. These examples don't aim to be a promotion of mastectomies, merely a reflection on how our social constructions (in this case medical institutions) draw lines regarding the modifications that a person is allowed to make to their bodies or not. Limits based on a corporal ethic that is sexist and gender essentialist. These restrictions are applied to all bodies, but only those who challenge them will come crashing up against these walls.

Gender Expression, Divine Treasure

Of all the concepts I've come across in recent years, one of the ones that interests me most is that of gender expression. It's the most useful tool I've encountered to promote gender diversity across different spheres. Gender expression can be masculine, feminine, androgynous, or whatever a person wants. It's a descriptive concept that tells us about the person's external and superficial presentation. When I say superficial I don't mean it in a negative sense, I'm merely referring to superficial in opposition to internal or subjective. That is to say, it doesn't give us information on how a person identifies but how their behavior is interpreted according to social norms. For example, when we say that a man is effeminate we are talking about his gender expression. We mean that his gender expression is feminine, but we're not saying anything about his body, his gender identity, or his sexual orientation. That is the first advantage of this concept: it's not an identity, but something other people attribute to us. It's purely descriptive and observational. It does not place a person in any category, it is not necessarily permanent and fixed for the person's entire life, no harsh judgment is applied. For example, a person may identify as a woman or a lesbian, but it is not as common for a woman to identify as masculine. Unlike "woman" (which is an identity category) or "lesbian" (which is a category of sexuality), "masculine" describes a person's gender expression but is not often seen as an identity in itself. Socially speaking, people don't think of "masculine women" as a collective, there are no associations of "masculine women," teens don't come out as "masculine women." In general, gender expression is something that others attribute to a person and not a category with which persons themselves identify. At least at this moment in time. That's not to say that a few years from now it won't emerge as an identifying category.

The second advantage of gender expression is that it has added important nuances to the classic sex/gender framework. To avoid confusion, I'm going to give a very didactic explanation. The classic sex/gender model holds sex and gender as the two main factors that determine the differences between men and women. "Sex" refers to a person's biology and there are two possibilities: male or female. Gender on the other hand refers to social behavior and has the same two options: masculine or feminine. The normative system we live in establishes that what is normal, natural, and healthy is that there should be a correlation between male sex and masculinity and between female sex and femininity. In recent years, this framework has been challenged and has become more nuanced. To explain this evolution I'd like to carry out a practical exercise using prominent figures in Spanish pop culture. Imagine if you had to complete the following sentence:

Falete is a person of _____ sex and _____ gender.

(If you don't know who Falete is, rush to Google now!) Most likely many people would fill those blanks in the following way: Falete is a person of male sex and feminine gender. Okay. Let's continue with the exercise. Now imagine you had to complete the following sentence:

Bibiana Fernández is a person of _____ sex and _____ gender.

Go ahead. Google it if you have to. Some people might short circuit because they don't want to be politically incorrect and for these people I'll make it easier: by sex I mean biological sex. With that said, you're most likely to answer in the following way: Bibiana Fernández is a person of male sex and feminine gender. This answer is also correct. Although many will have hesitated before responding that this person's sex is male, remember I said we were talking about biological sex. In both of these cases there is a lack of correspondence between sex and gender; they are crisscrossed. And in our society it is understood that people who have their sex and gender crisscrossed are effectively trans. Everything fits except one piece. These two people we are describing in fact have different experiences with their gender. Bibiana Fernández identifies as a woman whereas Falete identifies as a man but his gender expression is feminine. I'm not making this up. These two people have spoken publicly about their gender identities. But our model that only allows for two variables, sex and gender, overlooks this very important nuance. Both of these persons have male sex and feminine gender, but that would make it seem that they are both trans because in our social consciousness we think that when a person is very feminine it is obviously because they must feel like a woman inside, as if femininity were something exclusive to women.

To save ourselves these complications, it has been proposed that we add nuance to the sex/gender model. Now we talk about biological sex, gender identity, and gender expression. And everything becomes much clearer:

> Falete is a person of male biological sex, he identifies as a man, and his gender expression is female.

> Bibiana Fernández is a person of male biological sex, she identifies as a woman, and her gender expression is female.

(Again, please don't be offended by the fact that I've said a trans woman is of male biological sex. I'm referring to her original biology.)

The category "gender expression" does not claim to describe a person's essence but is more like a descriptive tool, a very valuable one. I consider it to be something like an oxygen tank for our way of thinking about gender norms because it offers a new and very interesting dimension. To start, we can talk about the fact that there are people with gender expressions that are different from their gender identities. Before, we could infer it, but we couldn't explain it in words. Now a person can explain that they feel like a man, even though they express themselves in a very feminine way according to our social codes. And this simple fact is very relevant from the trans perspective. It gives us the tools to explain for example how a child who was born as biologically male and yet has a very feminine gender expression could identify as a boy or as a girl. A feminine gender expression doesn't necessarily determine anything else. And what we urgently need is education on diversity of gender expression, to explain why people should be allowed to explore and express the entire range of gender expressions without that causing a conflict with respect to their gender identity. Or, to put it another way, gender identities should be able to house a broad range of possibilities, from extremely masculine to extremely feminine without that causing a conflict with respect to the person's identity. That would mean that we'd overcome the norm that assigns a strict gender expression to every gender identity. When that doesn't happen, when having a gender expression different to our gender identity causes conflict, that's when we ask ourselves: am I a man trapped in a woman's body? We ask ourselves this because we have such rigid gender identities that our actions, our practices, and our expressions keep us from fitting into the prescribed framework and we immediately think that the only logical thing to do is to modify our gender identities, through a gender transition.

A few days ago I discovered something that perfectly exemplifies the tension between gender identity and expression. It's a video by a YouTuber named King Yedet called *Am I*

Transsexual? At this point, she had not yet transitioned to living as a trans woman and still used male pronouns. In this video, he explained that from a young age he had always identified with femininity and women. These experiences had caused him to feel rejection and shame, and had led to many doubts about his gender identity. He also explained that everyone asked him if he was trans and that, after much thought and consideration, he had reached the conclusion that he was a feminine man. It seems simple, but things get complicated in this era of so many successful gender transitions. And he said that what helped him connect to himself and feel empowered to be himself was that a person very important to him validated his femininity even though he was a boy.

From my point of view, gender expression is the key piece in the sex–gender identity – gender expression – sexual orientation framework. Gender expression is the first thing we see when we meet someone and it's through this filter that we view all other categories. If a person's gender expression matches their biological sex we don't think any more about it. But when there is a mismatch we try to explain it by placing the person in other categories: they must be homosexual, they must be trans, etc. In our collective consciousness, extreme femininity in a boy has historically been an indicator of homosexuality and is seen today as an indicator of his being transgender. The typical reaction has always been to try to find an easy explanation for this person. He's feminine *because* of this or that. But now we propose simply accepting that we can't predict anything, that there's no way to know what choices a person will make later on, that it depends, it's subjective, that the boy is just feminine. Period. The boy simply has a feminine gender expression. If we are able to establish that a boy can have a very feminine gender expression, period, we'll have made major progress.

3

Photo Albums, Guerrillas, Cabarets, and Other Trenches. Activism as a Lifeline

Or as a Body-saver

How does a person go from wanting a surgery at all costs to deciding not to have any operation at all and even going nude on the beach despite having a different body? How does someone go from desperate to have an operation at all costs to desperate to save their body as if it were the most precious thing in the world? For me, trans activism has allowed me to experience my body in a more positive way, has provided a safe place from which to contemplate, has given me room to doubt, question, decide. That's why I'd like to share some of my story.

Photo Albums

I was thirteen years old the first time I entered a trans collective to ask for information. It was the CTC, the Col·lectiu de Transsexuals de Catalunya [Transsexuals Collective of Catalonia], which at that time met at the Casal Lambda in Barcelona. I went in alone, sat down, listened to the entire meeting and then left. What I heard there scared me so badly that it was a full year before I returned to another similar space.

It's not that they were hostile toward me; just the opposite. The members, mostly trans women, were very welcoming. But they were locked in very serious debates about the rights of sex workers, the limits of the term "transsexual," discrimination among trans people over whether a person wanted to have surgery or not, among many other things. I left terrified. Terrified at the thought of being someone like them in the midst of a wave of transphobia that I'd internalized. It terrified me to think of my body being operated on; I was terrified of all those things they talked about falling on top of me like an avalanche. I wanted to run away and that's basically what I did.

When I was ready to try again, a year later, I found a new space that had been created by a group of trans men, former members of the CTC, called Transsexual Men Group of Barcelona (GTMB for its initials in Spanish). And this time I stayed. Every Sunday I raced through the streets to the Gay Collective of Barcelona, which housed the weekly meetings of this small, magical family of trans boys, sometimes accompanied by their siblings, parents, partners, or friends. A place I would love to return to if it still existed, where I learned the immeasurable value of building support networks among trans people. I remember very vividly one of our favorite pastimes: looking at photographs of results of operations. It sounds surreal, but at that time it felt necessary. We would sit at a big table in the meeting room and open up the three-ring binders. Inside, like a photo album, were images of men, mostly from the United States, who had undergone mastectomies, hysterectomies, phalloplasties and other surgeries. Below each photo the name of the man was neatly printed, English names that sounded strange to us and were hard to pronounce (Bruce, Jack, Richard, Joe . . .) along with the date of their operation and the name of the surgeon. We commented on the images, compared them, and we imagined ourselves in their shoes. The lucky ones among us had already had an operation or two and recounted the process to us over and over, from pre-op to post-op, sparing no details. My favorite days were when someone had managed to tape an episode of a BBC documentary series about being transgender that aired in the middle of the night on Canal+. We plugged in a huge TV set that quickly swallowed the VHS and we watched in rapt silence. We almost always recognized the surgeons and almost never the anonymous protagonists. And that's how we spent every Sunday, eating sunflower seeds, laughing, and welcoming new members to the tribe. I was happy there in that group that was my oxygen after a week at school and I dreamed of being one of those boys in the photo album. I couldn't wait to have a body like theirs, and sharing my impatience made me feel lighter. But unlike the other members, I'd have a long time to wait because I was still a minor. It would be years before I could even get my diagnosis. So I waited, and in the meantime I participated in the shows of support from which I was never excluded, even though I was just a kid. I went to the hospital to visit friends as they woke up from anesthesia, accepted hand-me-down girdles (chest binders didn't exist at that time) from members who had finally been able to get rid of their breasts, and commiserated with those who woke up to discover that things hadn't gone so well, that their scars were huge, that they'd have to go back under the knife to redo something. All these experiences shaped my thoughts on corporal modification as I realized it was much less romantic than the photos had led us to believe.

Even though that time in my life seems distant to me now, I'm talking about the mid 2000s. It wasn't that long ago. More than a decade has passed, and in that time the trans movement has taken a giant leap forward.

Back then, the body was the epicenter of the debate. And I don't mean body positivity as an empowering idea but the body as testing grounds for surgical techniques as life-saving tools. I'd say that the debates we had at the GTMB were a snapshot of a very specific period (mid 2000s) in a specific context of the trans movement (the city of Barcelona). These debates sowed the seeds for a different way of approaching trans activism, although we didn't know it at the time. Despite the fact that bodily modification was an omnipresent topic of conversation at our meetings, there was something vitally important about those relationships, and it's that we never judged anyone for deciding to put their bodies through one process or another. No one was seen as more or less transgender (at that time the umbrella term "trans" didn't exist) for choosing to have an operation or not. Unlike what happened in other collectives of transgender persons (generally women), in which there were fierce debates about whether a non-operated trans woman should be considered a woman or even a transgender, the GTMB took a very different stance. I don't mean to imply that we were better: trans women discussed these issues with greater intensity because they were much more vulnerable to stigma and violence, making the issue of projecting a positive image in society essential. What I'm trying to say is that whatever one of us did with our bodies was not judged by other members and the safety of that environment allowed us to ask questions without fear of being exiled from the community.

The arrival of trans men on the trans activism scene in the late 1990s brought with it new ways of thinking about the work done by trans organizations. The main reason is probably that gender transitions for trans men had different implications: if we weren't talking about the same things as our female counterparts it's because we didn't have to combat the same stigma surrounding sex work or constant violence in the public sphere that they did.

Guerrillas

Then, in 2006, a pressing debate began within trans organizations across different parts of Spain, causing us to reconfigure everything. There was a major push for the passage of a law that would allow trans people to change their names on their ID cards. This was something that then-president José Luis Rodríguez Zapatero had promised the trans community, but his term was about to end and he had yet to enact the measure. So a group of activists decided to put forward an emergency proposal to try to get it passed before the upcoming elections. And they achieved their goal. We weren't accustomed to debating trans politics at the GTMB, we were more like a group of friends who supported each other emotionally. We were invested in each member's everyday adventures, but we'd never waded so deeply into legal issues and political strategies. The e-mail calling us to participate in the drafting of the law sparked internal debate, revealing our vastly different political stances. Some members of the group considered it a worthy cause and they went to Madrid to help work on the law, others thought the underlying proposal was totally unacceptable and needed to be discussed further. And that's how some of us sat down to create a critical response and ended up forming a new collective, the Guerrilla Travolaka [Trannie Guerillas]. A few months later, the GTMB definitively disbanded and our small family dispersed. But I still hold in my heart the memories, friendships, and experiences I had in that space, the best incubator for activism that I can imagine. I daresay that everyone who spent time there holds a profoundly loving memory of their experience.

The Guerrilla Travolaka started out as three trans guys, quickly joined by some lesbian activists, who were ready and willing to throw themselves into the project as much as or more than the rest of us. We didn't know how but we knew that we wanted to denounce the outsized role of doctors in decisions that so greatly impacted our lives as well as the perpetual medical treatment of trans people, which concealed an asphyxiating, normalizing gender system. The collective was frenetically active for three years and, when we finally halted our work, the seeds we'd sown sprouted into many other projects and initiatives that further disseminated our interpretation of the trans struggle. My time with the Travolakas was without a doubt one of the most brutal experiences in my life, because it represented a very deep rift between what I'd learned about trans people and what I began to experience. I'd say that this was when I began to feel that my body had been stolen from me, that we were being robbed of our bodies. I wasn't yet able to articulate this sensation in any coherent way; instead, it manifested as an overwhelming rage and acted as the driving force for our small but important activities that helped raise awareness for trans issues among other social movements in Barcelona.

For me personally there were two episodes that marked me profoundly and motivated me to join the Guerrilla Travolaka. Both occurred in France, where radical trans activists had been meeting for years. In July 2006 some of us made a pilgrimage to the Universités d'Été Euro-méditerranéennes des Homosexualités (UEEH), an event with a very long name created by radical lesbian, gay, trans, and intersex activists, which has been held every year since 1979 in Marseille, France. I never would have heard about it if I hadn't been invited by Karine Espineira, a French-Chilean activist and now a good friend. What I experienced there was transformative. More than 600 people from different countries participated in debates and assemblies, attended concerts and exhibitions. I suddenly found myself inside a bubble filled with trans activists from around the world, hearing empowering speeches that were very critical of the medical discourse and the psychiatrization of those who identified as transgender. I was awed, in total admiration, and I dreamed of the day that these political proposals might find their place in my hometown. The meetings were held in the Calanques Natural Park, a paradise of seaside cliffs and hidden beaches. And it was here that I experienced an awakening. As the final day drew near, a beach trip was planned. Groups of people, some of whom had known each other for years, but the majority for only a matter of days, began to prepare for the excursion. I wanted to go too. I wanted to participate in the group experience but, as I stumbled over the rocks, I was anxious about what I would do when I got to the water. Of course, I didn't plan on swimming, not if it meant exposing my body. And then I got to the beach. I didn't know what to expect but when I lifted my head and looked around, I saw a scene that would forever change me. Gender categories had disappeared. There were a thousand possible bodies, bodies I'd never seen before and which at the same time looked so similar to my own. Trans bodies in the water, dressed or naked, loud laughter and sunscreen everywhere. And, just like that, after so many hours, weeks, and months spent admiring the bodies of the boys in the three-ring binder, I suddenly found myself face to face with the exact opposite of what I'd imagined. I don't remember anything else about that day, I don't remember if I went swimming, I just remember that I was happy. I no longer wanted to be a boy like the ones in the photo album, I wanted to be like those people on the beach, wild and free, jumping from the rocks into the Mediterranean Sea. For the next nine summers I returned to these meetings and, yes, I eventually got into the water.

That same summer the French trans activists I'd just met (and fallen in love with) invited us to join Existrans, a trans rally in Paris, the following October. We immediately agreed. I couldn't stop thinking how great it would be to have something like that in Barcelona, where trans visibility was practically non-existent and we needed to do something about it. These experiences motivated me to return home and work nonstop with our small guerrilla trans group toward this goal. Six months later our French trans friends came to Barcelona to help us with great enthusiasm and generosity. And a month later, in October 2007, Barcelona hosted the first trans rally in all of Spain.

Although the Guerrilla Travolaka's main objective was to denounce the pathologization of transgenderism, a challenge to bodily modification can be read between the lines in the group's manifesto, in which we said:

> [. . .] We defend Doubt, we believe in "going backwards" medically as a way of moving forward. We believe that no process of construction should be labeled *irreversible*. We want to shine a light on the beauty of androgyny. We believe in the right to remove our bandages and breathe easy as well as the right to keep them on, in the right to good surgeons and not *butchers*, in free access to hormonal treatments without a certificate from any psychiatrist, in the right to self-administer hormones. We demand the right to live without asking for permission [. . .]

This excerpt denounces blind acceptance of the medical model and defends bodily autonomy. And, although it may seem that essentially what is being defended is the right to modify the body, it is also defending the body that does not desire modification, the body that remains androgynous. Another example can be found in the campaign launched in April 2007, in which we coined the expression "gender euphoria." This was a series of photographs with political slogans that had the objective of denouncing the medicalization implied in the so-called Gender Identity Law passed on March 15, 2007. In the text that accompanied the campaign we said: "We believe in – and live with – bodies that are not taking hormones, intersex, transgender. We have what you are so afraid of: breasts and penises, vaginas and beards." One of the captions for the images, which showed a naked torso with mastectomy scars, read: "Are my scars masculine?" The aim was to challenge the public as to why a surgically altered torso was seen as something preferable when at the end of the day it was still far from the prototypical male torso. The campaign in general and this image in particular represented a clear denouncement of the obligation to modify the body, but at the time they didn't receive as much attention as other slogans, such as "Why do I have to ask the doctor for permission?" These images were later used by many other campaigns against trans pathologization in Spain. We prioritized this message and the issue of the body remained in the background, although it was still important. This is what "gender euphoria" meant to us, a denouncement of the pathologizing category of "gender dysphoria," the term used to label us in medical journals and even by Spanish law at the time. The euphoria we felt was huge and it implied the celebration of gender and body diversity. Today we see the expression "gender euphoria" used in many contexts, often very distant from its original sense. But we'll talk more about that later.

We worked hard over those three years. In June 2007 we held the first ever protest against pathologization outside the Gender Identities Disorder Unit of the Hospital Clinic of Barcelona. There were exactly forty of us, of which almost half came from neighboring countries. Our message was not popular *at all*, not even among trans people. In parallel, we held dozens of events and gatherings such as the Kafetas Travolakas [Trannie Dinner Parties], Cómete al Psikiatra [Eat the Psychiatrist], or the Santa Wilfrida Masses, where we celebrated our resistance, celebrated being ourselves despite the pressures to be something else. We decorated vans to attend protests with logos that read: Gender Moving Co. or Gender Trapeze Artists Circus. We held conferences, created a trans film festival, the Mostra'ns. We organized in conjunction with national and international activists to hold trans manifestations simultaneously in different cities every October. And finally, in the summer of 2009, we created an international campaign that is still in existence today called Stop Trans Pathologization, which invites trans activists in cities all over the world to take to the streets every October to denounce trans pathologization in its various expressions. But, looking back now, one of the most important things we did was to let ourselves be influenced by feminist discourses, ideas that nourished and stimulated our critical view of the trans reality.

We also cared for one another deeply. I suppose that's why we ended up parting ways. But everything we'd learned stayed with us. The collectives, projects, and initiatives that each one of us later formed have drawn from that guerrilla inheritance we are so proud of.

Cabarets

Radical trans activism felt like a romantic adventure to me, but it was not without its detractors. Many people who defined themselves as transgender considered our political proposal to be ridiculous. Their opposition was often expressed with extreme belligerence, but the dissenting voices did force me to examine our position critically and reflect on the work we'd been doing. The conclusion I came to then was that, however radical our proposals, they were not effective in transforming the collective consciousness of trans people. That wouldn't have been enough of a reason for me to abandon radicalism, but the fact that so many trans people saw us as their enemies made me stop and think. I don't mean to say that I agreed with the transgender activists who demonized us. In many cases I think it was more of a battle for political space, which some of the movement's veterans were unwilling to cede to new ways of understanding the trans experience (something that has happened in the history of all social movements). But, apart from those voices, I realized that there was a distrust and lack of comprehension from many of the trans people with whom we came into contact.

Something very similar had occurred not far removed from the Barcelona trans activist scene a few years prior. In 2001 a few French trans activists had joined together to form GAT (Groupe Activiste Trans) [Trans Activist Group]. The collective developed a plan for very innovative direct actions within the European trans movements with tactics inspired by the ACT UP movement for the fight against AIDS. The majority of their actions were centered on denouncing the psychiatrization of trans people. Their work made an impact and, for me, without a doubt, they were very inspiring. But the reality is that, despite becoming a reference point for more radical trans activism, GAT also had many detractors, especially in the trans community. The constant criticisms undermined them to the point that, in 2006, exhausted from constantly having to justify and defend themselves, they decided to dissolve. To make it public they circulated a communique that was also not without controversy. It was entitled *A Trans Community?* and it said the following:

> When GAT formed there were four of us: four angry trans people. Four anarchists. We dreamed of a revolution. Of freedom. Of depsychiatrization. You thought there were thousands of us. You were wrong. You claimed you were members of GAT. You lied to yourselves. No one joins GAT just as no one quits GAT. It's a rule. It's our rule. We were born in secret in 2001. We've decided we will die publicly in 2006. An intentionally ephemeral structure. We won't say any more about our withdrawal from the public space, we will let you form your own criticisms, predictions, interpretations, and determinations. We have rejected the words of psychiatrists who dare to speak and write in our names. You have criticized the symbolic violence of our actions. We've railed against government power. You've censured our radicalism. We've politically demanded depsychiatrization. You've denied the urgency of the situation, the need for a revolution. We've publicly denounced our enemies. You've chosen silence, disregard, victimization, guilt, and shame. You've taken us for fools. You are puppets in a system you have chosen to support, keeping your mouths shut. We have fought over territory, faced down those who would

oppress us. You've taken refuge in theory. We were warriors. Incorruptible. You continue to negotiate with the enemy.

We have fought the system. you have preferred to fight us.[1]

As a deep lament, GAT's last communication was a harsh criticism of the trans community itself, by which they felt abandoned and misunderstood and even betrayed. Despite the fact that this occurred in France, GAT's message caused me to seriously question my own experience. I understood their rage, of course, but I didn't agree that responsibility for their failure should fall to the trans community (which according to them didn't even exist). Maybe it sounds identitarian, but I would say that trans people should not be our main enemy. Even if we sometimes feel that beyond the fact of having all gone through a gender transition we don't have anything in common with trans people who repeat essentialist, conservative discourses, I'd say that we shouldn't get our enemies confused. Of course, I think that we can and should challenge positions that we don't agree with, but I think it's important to look to the power structures and systems that uphold these positions to begin with. If we truly want to transform the consciousness surrounding trans people, we need to be able to question it, even if it doesn't feel good. I have a lot of respect for the GAT collective and I also think we can learn a lot from their ultimate failure.

As I was focused on these reflections, our local trans scene began to grow and branch out in several different directions: the fight for the depathologization at the institutional level, the articulation of transfeminism, and the defense of trans as the maximum expression of the gender revolution. I'd say that 2010 was the peak of the soufflé of trans radicalism and I felt increasingly that I didn't identify with what was happening around me. Something didn't fit, we couldn't possibly embody

---

[1] Originally in French.

the trans revolution if we were so widely rejected by the broader trans community. The conferences we organized and the protests we orchestrated were attended by radical activists but very few trans people. And the problem was that our political proposal was a good one but we weren't explaining it properly (kind of like GAT). So I exited by the fire escape and tried to start over.

It was a state of emergency: we were being robbed of our bodies. (In fact, it's still a state of emergency.) So a small group of activists decided to once again get to work and create a project especially centered on giving coverage and visibility to a diversity of trans figures, discourses, and bodily experiences with which trans people could identify. The objective was to create initiatives that were welcoming, so that trans people who were beginning their transition could see diverse ways of being trans without feeling judged by their decisions. The hope was that some people might be inspired by these alternatives. That's how the Cultura Trans [Trans Culture] project was born in 2011 and it remains active today, coordinated by myself, along with Pol Galofre, incomparable brother-in-arms. I'd say that the project has worked; we changed our way of reaching out to people and the people who approached us changed as a result. Trans people slowly began to attend our activities until they finally became the majority of the regular attendees. I see Cultura Trans as an iron giant that we are constructing bit by bit as a mechanism of resistance. Sitting there in the audience, I've watched many trans people recounting extraordinary, revelatory, daring, emotional, liberating experiences. I could go on. Personally it has been a constant source of inspiration and a great aid in helping me build a better relationship with my own body. One of my favorite activities has been the Trans Dialogues, a space in which six or seven different trans people answer the same three questions. It's all available on the internet but I'd like to highlight a few, such as Joana López, who said:

I think that we have to empower ourselves. We have to be proud of our bodies just the way they are. To know that our bodies have some limits, that we're never going to be masculine to the max or feminine to the max. That we're going to reach a limit and stop there.

Or a reflection made by Keops Guerrero:

I think it's important to know that we have a body, we have a biology that we're born with, that we have to be very clear about that and very aware of it. And with that body as the base we can do a thousand things. We have to accept our bodies and what we were dealt . . . I think that if we can do that we're going to be fuller and we're going to have less conflict.

Also the words of Sabrina Sánchez:

Just last year I went to a nude beach and I didn't take off my bottoms. This year I said: Look, we're all different. There are people who are fatter, thinner, taller, shorter. Why the hell can't there be a girl with a penis? Let people get used to it.

And Martina Nikolle's thoughts:

The only problem I've discovered now is that I sometimes want to have surgery and sometimes I don't, it's a dilemma: how can I be sure that I want to have this surgery because it's something I'm genuinely unhappy with, a problem I have inside me that causes me discomfort when I meet other people or is it just what I want other people to see? And this question keeps coming up all the time, and it's what stops me every time I think I want to change my body.

There are hours and hours of recordings by many very wise, generous people who dare to defy trans normativity and share their doubts surrounding the myth of the wrong body. People talk about how their experiences with dance, sex work, traditional Japanese medicine, or swimming have helped them reconcile with their bodies. Or, translated into the language of this book, people who have resisted the robbery of their bodies and are willing to share the tools they used.

But without a doubt the most popular event hosted by Cultura Trans is the Trans Art Cabaret. This crazy idea started out in the emblematic Diables de Sant Andreu (probably the most generous people in Barcelona) and spread to theatres where they let us wreck their "artistic vision" for the cause. (Damned theatres and their "artistic visions.") The Trans Art Cabaret has become an annual event in which professional and amateur trans artists take to the stage to express themselves through various scenic arts before an enraptured audience. At first it was just our friends, now total strangers reserve tickets via the internet weeks in advance. The Cabaret is almost a ritual celebration of trans resistance and trans bodies and a chance to prove that trans people can do extraordinary things with their hands, their voices, their feet, their presence, and their words.

Something else we resumed after our post-radical reflective pause were the meetings of the Espai Trans [Trans Space]. This space for trans people to meet and socialize was first created in 2008 but that early incarnation never really took off, perhaps because we didn't fully believe in it. But gathering with other trans people felt truly essential; our political position wouldn't make any sense otherwise. We didn't want to continue creating things only a few of us would see, but to build networks among trans people so that we could all live better. And, personally, I dearly missed the Sunday afternoon meetings of the Grup de Transsexuals Masculins [Transsexual Mens Group]. It took a while but, after much effort, patience, and care, the Espai Trans meetings began to draw a crowd. Some Fridays there are as many as thirty trans people gathered there. It's a place to make friends, flirt, start new collectives, and form chosen families. All of this restored our confidence in the notion that mutual support networks and spaces for peers to gather are essential to our trans community. It's not enough merely to make radical proposals: you have to take care of people, listen to them talk again and again (a thousand and one times) about their desperation over not being able to have surgery, the conflicts they feel, their challenges with the professionals at the Gender Unit of the public hospital, and their fears over flirting with someone at a club. All of that is very important. And, as time passes, these same people may tell you that they still want to have an operation, but they no longer feel so rushed, or that they've found another place to get hormones, or they flirted with someone at a nightclub. And then that Friday was worth it. The Espai Trans, which had its tenth anniversary in 2018, is the only fixed meeting space for trans people in Catalonia. The event is fantastic but, if I'm honest, there are also a lot of things we could improve: we've never been able to capture the spirit of those Sunday afternoons. It's hard to recreate that family atmosphere because people come intermittently, and every month we have to go through a dizzying round of introductions. But we see ourselves as feeling our way through, building a foundation so that other trans people might be able to tear it down and rebuild it in the future. (Because according to the trans teens we're already over the hill.) We're open to suggestions (wink).

Other Trenches

In February 2018 some of us wanted to commemorate the ten-year anniversary of the first trans protest in Barcelona, so we decided to organize a conference series titled *Una re-vuelta trans* [*A Trans Re-volution*]. The response was overwhelming and, looking back now, it is clear that the critical trans struggle in Barcelona over the last decade has created a kaleidoscope of alliances, initiatives, and projects.

I feel that it's important to recount this journey for several reasons. First of all, I want to be able to explain to future generations of trans people what the hell we were doing while our bodies were being robbed. Well, we were doing the best we could, we weren't sitting around twiddling our thumbs. And, secondly, I think stories have to be told; a Facebook timeline is not enough. So this is my small contribution to the researchers of trans history, my attempt to make it easier for them than it was for me to discover our roots. Telling our own story is another important battle because up to now others have always told it for us. Thirdly, it was in this context that the tide flooded in. When trans visibility inundated the media as never before in history and everyone began to jump for joy over transphobia being banished from the face of the earth, while all that was happening, some of us were doing other, smaller things. It caught us by surprise. Or, more like, it caught us very busy.

Part II

The Flood

4

Trans is Pop

At a glance, it would appear that the trans movement is having an incredible moment. The emergence of so many trans references and discourses in the media opens a new debate on how the model of empowerment is improving the trans experience in general and a respect for the bodies of trans people specifically. Until very recently, trans invisibility was extremely problematic. And, in a very short period of time, the scene has changed completely.

It is in the midst of this flood of trans visibility that it seems relevant that we ask ourselves some questions. What caused this? What has changed in the last two or three years that has led to such visibility for trans people in our society? Why? Which people have received greatest attention? And above all, how are trans people's bodies depicted in these media representations? Many trans activists are obsessed by questions such as these. From my point of view, what is being popularized is a very narrow and specific understanding of trans which, when examined closely, has many underlying problems.

Without a doubt, this tide of trans visibility has also allowed for the emergence of interesting narratives and discourses that are critical of trans normativity and celebrate gender diversity.

The wave has washed many new trans references onto the shores of our collective consciousness. Nevertheless, I'd say that some of these references have left a deeper imprint than others and certain stories have become the new hegemonic narrative of the trans experience.

In this chapter I would like to analyze these narratives critically, to think about the ways in which they have managed to stand out in this recent surge of media visibility and to pick apart the discourses they put forward and values they promote.

Within this torrent of trans stories I'd say there are two main narratives that have been proffered as examples of new trans empowerment. On one hand, we have the "trans women with heroic journeys and respectable professions," and on the other we have "transgender minors." What about trans men, you might ask; why aren't they represented in this new trans visibility? Let's not kid ourselves: trans men have never played in the same league as trans women. In our collective consciousness, trans boys do not face as much social or professional exclusion, so they don't have such a desperate need to be normalized. (And no, I'm not insinuating that trans men have never experienced transphobia, just that their symbolic representation in the social consciousness was never that of the total marginalization trans women have experienced but merely relative invisibility and latent lesbophobia.)

Getting back to the matter at hand, let's dive deeper into these two types of narratives, starting with "trans women with heroic journeys and respectable professions," a popular plotline in the US media.

Trans is Pop

The US trans activist Julia Serano explains in her article "*Skirt* Chasers: Why the Media Depicts the Trans Revolution in Lipstick and Heels" that trans women in the movies can almost always be described in one of two ways: deceptive or pathetic. The deceptive trans woman is an attractive heterosexual woman, totally invisible as a trans person to the naked eye, who seeks to seduce men by hiding her past. At the end of these movies it is discovered that she is truly a trans woman and she is suddenly seen as despicable for daring to lie about something so essential and most of all for having threatened male heterosexuality. A fairly negative portrayal, to be certain. The pathetic trans woman, in contrast, is fully visible as a trans woman and is presented as overdone, obsessed with femininity to the point of absurdity. She will never pass unnoticed as a woman, so she is not a threat to heterosexual men, who will never "fall into her trap." Again, a fairly negative characterization. For decades, the representation of trans women has been lazy, stereotypical, and far from empowering. But it would seem that the media representation has recently changed and we now see inspiring stories of successful trans people. The deceptive/pathetic dichotomy has opened up and a new framework is now needed to analyze the avalanche of modern trans characters.

Surely the most paradigmatic case due to the media attention she has garnered is Caitlyn Jenner, a trans woman who introduced herself to the world on the cover of *Vanity Fair* in 2015. Jenner is neither deceptive nor pathetic. She is what you could call "a trans woman with a heroic journey and respectable profession," the new prototype. Other women we could add to this group are director Lana Wachowski, ex-soldier Chelsea Manning, and actress Laverne Cox, among other figures. I am aware that these last three trans women I've just cited have been openly critical of social inequality and have shown an authentic commitment to the trans community and social justice issues (unlike Jenner, who encouraged people to vote for Donald Trump). But what I want to focus on is not so much their stories as their representations in the media, which is often beyond their control. That is to say, I respect what they are doing, artistically or politically, but I'm uncomfortable with the way the mass media has tamed and softened their images. Manning was on the cover of *Vogue* in 2017, Cox on the cover of *TIME* in May 2014. How is that possible? Why them? Why now?

Some of you might be thinking that I should just be happy about it, that I should be jumping for joy, that positive stories of trans people appearing in the media is great news. But I think it's a much more delicate issue. It's true that an increase in trans stories enriches our collective consciousness. But that doesn't mean we can't critically analyze these new references. Beyond the trans narrative that they present, however positive it may be, what interests me are the underlying vales being promoted. So let's try something: before we start jumping for joy, let's take a careful look at these stories. And then we can determine whether there's cause for joy.

More than ten years ago something appeared on Spanish television that made more than one trans man consider the risks of visibility controlled by the mass media. It was 2005 and male transgender visibility was practically null. People didn't know that we even existed or what we looked like. And then, on that year's edition of *Big Brother*, the show's casting directors chose a trans man as a participant. His name was Niki; we can all agree that he was the first trans man to ever become well known by a mainstream Spanish television audience. People said to us "You must be so happy! Finally a trans guy on TV! This is going to be so important to showing people your reality!" And we were left scratching our heads and trying to avoid the topic so that we wouldn't come across as sour, curmudgeonly activists who, worst of all, were ungrateful.

Niki represented the most classical masculine values: aggression, sexism, intolerance, etc. And, as the first trans man on TV, well it didn't exactly make me want to set off fireworks in celebration. Rumor has it that *Big Brother* held a separate casting call specifically to recruit trans people for the show. I cringe to think whom they rejected. For a long time, at almost every talk and roundtable, I answered questions about the infamous Niki and what he meant for the visibility of trans men in the social consciousness. And when I gave an honest opinion, I always received the same reaction: "Well, would you rather have Niki or nothing?" It's a trick question. The point is not to censure certain stories or keep them from being told on television but to recognize the impact that one story will have when there are no other visible narratives. There's the risk of generating a stereotype, a single narrative. It's about trans visibility and trans role models: if there are many different kinds of trans stories in the media there will be a rich narrative, but if we only get one single role model, I'd say that the values they promote are crucial.

I share this anecdote to contextualize the perspective of trans activism. We've always been trapped in this false dilemma of whether we should prefer representation mediated by TV stations over nothing at all. And we've learned the hard way to be critical of the role models assigned for us. We know we can aspire to something better. It is crucial to consider carefully the stories, narratives, and values expressed when presenting characters or persons whose representation in the social imaginary is non-existent. Of course there has to be diversity, but when there's nothing to start with, there also has to be some sense of responsibility. In a society in which people can name at least five trans men, then you can throw Niki into the ring. In a society in which people don't even know that gender transitions can go both ways, having Niki as the only reference is irresponsible. What I want to say is that misrepresentation is not an acceptable alternative to zero representation. Just because trans people are invisible doesn't mean we're required to accept any visibility as a positive and we don't have to feel thankful when we hear supposedly amazing stories like Caitlyn Jenner's. Just the opposite; we should never lose our willingness to analyze and question the values being promoted by those figures. In short: simply being trans is not enough for a trans role model to be a positive one. It's not enough at all. María Dolores Cospedal and Angela Merkel are women and they are not enough for feminism.

Trans activism has to remain critical of the role models presented and to view them from an intersectional perspective. It's not enough to get a little bit of trans acceptance and then we can all go home. Because, if so, we'd be on our way home soon. Trans acceptance in broad strokes is just around the corner. But we have to go much further than that, which means we have to abandon identitarian thinking. We can't focus solely and exclusively on recognition for the trans community without linking this social transformation to other demands. It's likely that, if we only concern ourselves with trans visibility, we will only make visible a specific type of trans person: with a certain skin color, a certain amount of resources, a certain level of socioeconomic capital, and certain values surrounding gender. And, as we gain social recognition for this one type of trans person, we further marginalize other groups of trans people. To break with this logic we have to understand that the kind of violence that trans people experience is articulated in a complex set of systems that generates inequalities and violence to different degrees. And, therefore, transforming our social system doesn't happen solely and exclusively through the social inclusion of trans people, but through a questioning of the system itself. How can trans role models benefit us if they are also racist, classist, and sexist? Where do more radical trans people stand, or trans sex workers, or working-class trans people? What do we think when other movements promote role models who may further their causes but are transphobic at the same time? In this sense, the work of trans activist and lawyer Dean Spade (2015) is, in my opinion, one of the most brilliant recent contributions to critical and intersectional trans politics.

Returning to the analysis of trans role models, some years ago I attended a conference organized by activist Antonio

Centeno, who works toward visibilizing the sexuality of persons with functional diversity/disabilities. Centeno proposed a very interesting analysis of his community's social recognition, specifically the ways our society configures men with disabilities. Basically there are three possible narratives: "the man that doesn't want to live so he fights for assisted suicide," see Ramón Sampedro; "the genius man who makes important scientific discoveries," see Stephen Hawking; or "the superhero who overcomes obstacles through strength of spirit to be able to walk again," see Christopher Reeve. These media personalities certainly offer visibility, but what kind of visibility is it and what values does it imply? Centeno argued that, if you don't want to die, you're not a genius, but you also don't have any hope of getting better, it's very hard to find your place (interview in Sales and Tasias 2012). This triad of prototypes reminded me of Serano's dichotomy of the pathetic/deceptive trans woman and it made me wonder if we weren't merely adding on another category. The new figure is a heroine, similar to the disabled man who overcomes all odds that Centeno talked about. And how did these women come to be seen as heroines? Why them and not the trans women who came before them? My hypothesis is that there's a power structure holding them all up: the novelty is not that they are trans women; what is unexpected or new is the economic, cultural, and social capital that they have accumulated.

In the 1970s in Spain, the first generations of trans women carried out their transitions at a relatively young age. When they entered the labor market they did so as trans women and, in the majority of cases, they experienced social exclusion due to their gender transition. When they tried to enter the labor market they had no possibility of developing any minimally recognized professional trajectory, so a large number of them turned to entertainment or sex work, more than dignified work to be certain but work that in our hypocritical society is highly stigmatized, adding to their existing marginalization due to being visible trans women. In fact, this is still the reality for many trans women, especially migrants.

The trans women who have recently emerged as trans role models in the media have very different stories. The main difference is that they underwent their transition at an older age, after establishing respectable careers and more comfortable social positions (Jenner was an elite athlete, Manning became known as a soldier and intelligence analyst for the US military, and Wachowski was already a successful director). This explains how they gained socio-economic positions that so few trans women ever achieve, the trick is that they gained their status when they lived as men and from that social position they initiated gender transitions. Their trans journey has undoubtedly impacted their social standing and their professional opportunities, but it has not pushed them into social exclusion. I'm not trying to pass moral judgment on the paths they've taken, merely to consider why these stories have received so much media attention whereas previous trans women's stories have not. And I conclude that one of the main reasons for the huge media interest in these particular trans stories is these women's social class.

5

Trojan Horses in a Trans Revolution

The year 2015 saw not only Caitlyn Jenner on the cover of *Vanity Fair*, it was also the year that the Spanish public discovered transgender minors. What I mean is that the category "transgender minor" began to gain visibility, organizations were formed, the mothers and fathers of trans youths were invited to the morning television and radio programs to tell their stories, and so on. In the paragraphs that follow I will attempt to explain how the narrative constructed by organizations in defense of transgender minors in Spain has introduced a new way of configuring the trans struggle that is in stark opposition to certain strands of trans activism. To better explain myself, I'd like to base my criticism around three central points: the new category that these movements have created, the theory on gender identity that they promote, and the relationship to the body that they establish.

And, before the police officers out there start with the "Shut up, you don't speak for me, you're usurping my voice," let me clarify two things: first of all, I was once a "transgender minor" (some of us trans adults began their transitions before age eighteen), and secondly and much more importantly, I think it's worth listening to everyone, no matter their gender identity.

I'd also like to state once again that the objective of this book is to reflect critically on current trans politics and how they relate to the body. The intention is not to judge anyone's experiences or the decisions that trans people and their families have made specifically, but simply to discuss the underlying theoretical paradigms. I repeat this because I've often felt that it's nearly impossible to talk about this issue without being suspected of transphobia. But building a wall around trans politics so that no one can question them out of fear of being accused of transphobia is not at all conducive to a rich political debate.

The Emergence of Trans Minors: A New Identity

First of all, I'd like to begin by recognizing that the emergence of the "transgender minor" category has been crucial to starting the conversation about the gender discomfort felt by persons under the age of eighteen. At the same time, as happens with the creation of any category, it has laid the foundation for a new possible identity.

Similarly, the creation of the categories "gay," "lesbian," "bisexual," or "transgender" transformed what before were specific practices into identities in themselves. That is to say, before these terms were coined, a man who slept with another man was practicing homosexual behavior; today he is a homosexual. This concrete practice converts him into a type of person, a gay man, and implies that being gay means many more things than a simple sexual preference. Being gay is associated in our culture with a multitude of stereotypes such as a certain relationship to art, specific sensibilities and aesthetics, femininity, and even a determined relationship with their mother. This idea I've just roughly outlined here is developed in much greater detail by the French philosopher Michel Foucault in *The History of Sexuality* (1992), but basically I wanted to point out the essentialism that these identities establish.

In the case at hand, the emergence of the category "transgender minor" has generated the identity "transgender minor." That is to say that, today, there are children who *are* transgender minors, it's something you are or you are not. It's a limited, defined, closed identity. And to my mind that's one of the more problematic issues caused by the emergence of this category. It seems to me much more interesting to approach the suffering of gender in childhood and adolescence through a critical perspective of gender norms. This would allow us to think of experiences in relation to gender as a range of possibilities, in constant evolution, that may be closer or more distant to the social norm and therefore exposed to greater or lesser degrees of violence. But of course having a diverse gender expression doesn't put a person into a category different to the rest of the boys and girls in their class. That logic draws a line between different forms of experiencing gender: the "normative" and the "transgender" (a dichotomy that doesn't make much sense, given that childhood is characterized by non-normative gender expressions).

Additionally, the category itself is founded on two concepts that are fiercely and widely debated: the category "minor" and the category "transgender." I'm not going to take a deep dive into the criticism that they have received, but I will point out a couple that seem to me most relevant. The first problem is that it seems very risky to unify under a single umbrella all persons from age zero to age eighteen. The shifting relationship between identity and gender expression throughout all of childhood and adolescence cannot be viewed from one single lens, as if the development of subjectivity itself does not take giant leaps between childhood and adolescence. But I believe that the problems with the category "transgender minor" go well beyond gender. The second issue is that identifying as transgender is an adult concept in itself: its origin and the treatments that have been developed are configured in relation to an adult age. It is a declaration of desiring to live a different gender identity in a constant and irreversible way, often through explicitly altering the body. I'm not necessarily defending these criteria but, if we're going to choose to use the term "transgender," which is a medical category, we should understand its history and its limitations.

If "minor" is a legal category and "transgender" a medical one, "transgender minor" is a legal–medical category. As I've said, the choice of these terms to define this experience seems confusing and problematic from the outset. But, someone might say, even if the category is founded on two dubious concepts, in practice it is much broader and more varied. So I'd like to take a moment to reflect on how this category has emerged and the theoretical framework it proposes to describe this reality.

The Discovery of Transgender Minors or the Colonization of Gender Diversity

In my opinion, the intense focus placed on transgender minors has hijacked trans movements and politics. It seems that a false dichotomy has been established in which, if a person doesn't agree with what is being said by the organizations in support of trans minors, they are nothing short of transphobic and ruthlessly endangering the rights of children. Something like "you're either with me or you're transphobic," rejecting the existence of any other ways of configuring gender experiences in childhood and adolescence.

When I was a child, I was once made to color some ships at school in honor of the 500-year anniversary of the "discovery" of America. Columbus arrived, "discovered" these lands, which before him had been nothing, and he created a civilized place called the New World. Half a millennia later we celebrated this by coloring the *Niña*, the *Pinta*, and the *Santa María* at school. The recent boom of transgender minors reminds me of the "discovery" of the New World. If no one had come in to write on the chalkboard about these little creatures with little legs and little arms called transgender minors we never would have known about them. The official narrative presupposes that before, there was nothing, only silence; we were blind and we didn't see that there were these little people with their own rights who were being ignored, misunderstood, and even oppressed.

The movements for the decolonization of the Americas pointed out that what occurred was not a discovery but an occupation. One group of people wiped out something that had existed for a long time to impose their understanding of civilization. But without going as far as genocidal colonization, there is also cultural colonization, through media, scientific, and institutional discourses. And something similar to this happens with transgender minors: trans activism has tried to explain that before the creation of this new category, there were people working in different ways to address the issue from a critical perspective, there were families dealing with gender diversity the best they could. There were children growing up struggling to fit into one of the rigid gender identities available to them. I refuse to believe that with the creation of this new category we have suddenly achieved peace and salvation from the hell of the past. There are other possible versions of what happened before. The fact that this model, to be followed when dealing with transgender minors, is presented as a truth and not as one possible path gives us many clues as to the type of discourse it furthers.

Boys with feminine gender expressions and girls with masculine gender expressions have probably always existed. What is new is the labeling of these children as transgender minors. What's novel is the identity category used to define these behaviors. That doesn't mean transgender minors have always existed and we've just now learned how to see them but that transgender minors exist as far as the category exists. Before, they couldn't exist because we couldn't even think in those terms, so there were other possibilities.

Until recently, childhood wasn't a period in which the category of transgender could be attributed to anyone. It was taken as a given that any decision about a gender transition would be made in adulthood (or perhaps adolescence). And this way of approaching the question of gender diversity had its pros and its cons. On the negative side, the lack of acceptance of diverse gender expression in childhood could lead to profound suffering and violence. On the positive side, these experiences weren't labeled with a fixed identity and therefore children weren't predestined to a specific identitarian path. I'm not implying that the way families dealt with these experiences before was in any way better, just that the range of possibilities in their minds was broader than it is today.

Before, when the category of "transgender minor" did not yet exist, there were in general two typical reactions from family members: one model, in which the families punished those gender expressions in their children, rejected them, or even exercised violence against them; and a second model, in which the families provided support that required a necessary flirting with uncertainty. And this second model is the one I'm especially interested in and would like to reflect on.

In the logic of these families, when a boy was very feminine, or even identified as a girl, they might think something like "maybe he'll grow up to be gay." And a possible identity was projected into the future, with no certainty beyond a prudent intuition. However, current discourses on childhood transgenderism maintain that the correct thing to do is to determine definitively whether this child is in fact a transgender girl and, in that case, act now to lay the groundwork for a process of transition. And it is precisely this perspective that seems risky to me. If we compare these two approaches (the one where the families don't ascribe any one identity to these behaviors and the one where being transgender is hypothesized), I don't see how the first is worse than the second. I don't consider the first option to be blind and the second to be the enlightened truth. I don't see that the first family has a non-identified transgender girl. If that were the case, we would be surrounded by people who were not identified in childhood as transgender. Many adults had gender expressions that were in opposition to their assigned gender when they were children. What's more, many of these people who were not identified as trans chose other paths and today they are simply feminine men or masculine women.

But I'd like to go a little further: not only does it seem to me that the families who don't label their kids as trans aren't worse, I think that they are creating a more open environment for their children to freely make choices, and a more positive environment, in relation to their children's bodies and sexualities. This comparison might seem unfair because the two models were created in different historical contexts and therefore with different understandings of gender and identity. But even today, there are still families actively deciding to support their children without associating specific gender behaviors to transgender identity in childhood. This is currently happening, even though it's not easy because the hegemonic narrative pushes people toward labeling any uncertainty as transgenderism.

I'll return to these ideas later to refute the notion that any critical analysis of transgender minors is based in transphobia, but first I want to challenge the prevailing narrative and propose an alternative that allows for other possible ways of supporting our children.

Sleeping with the Enemy

Despite the problems with the identity category "transgender minor" itself, and specifically the ways in which it has unfurled in Spain, some might still say that the proposal is interesting and empowering. It's true that I have not yet laid out the content of this proposal and it's worth giving it a chance.

When I finally paused to take a closer look at the way the discourses on trans minors related to broader trans issues I received an unpleasant surprise. The sensation I came away with was that the debate over trans minors has facilitated a forceful return to the same old discourses on identifying as transgender that trans activists had been fighting against. For a brief moment, it had seemed that we'd managed to establish that psychiatrists, endocrinologists, and surgeons did not have the final word as the utmost experts on transgenderism. That's basically what the struggle for trans depathologization was about. But with the emergence of the category "transgender minor" came new medical experts, new discourses surrounding sex in the brain and the innatism of being transgender. This is evidenced in the many celebrated documentaries on trans minors that have aired on public television, where doctors played a starring role. I'd like to share some excerpts from "El sexo sentido," which aired on the program *Documentos TV* on Channel 2 on June 15, 2014: "Just as organisms, our entire bodies, develop in one direction, toward male or female, the same thing also happens in the brain. And that's what we're studying in transgender persons" (Antonio Guillamón, director of Psychobiology, UNED). And, "Today neuroscience is teaching us that we are born with a male or female brain and that, no matter how much the culture or society exerts pressure, no matter how many surgeries are done, you will never change that sexual orientation" (Iván Mañero, plastic, reconstructive, and aesthetic surgeon). Or this other example from "Transit," aired on the program *30 minuts* on TV3 on April 6, 2016:

A transgender person is born transgender. It seems there is some anomaly that occurs in the first trimester of gestation, which is when the sexualization of the body and brain occurs.

There are many theories. None of them has been scientifically proven, but yes, the one that seems to get closest says that there's some hormonal anomaly that occurs that causes the brain and body to be differentiated sexually. So the brain sexualizes as female, for example, and the body as male. From there this person will become a transgender woman, because their body will be male but their brain will be female and they will identify as female. (Teresa Godás, psychologist. Gender Identity Unit of the Hospital Clinic of Barcelona)

Prominent organizations of transgender minors and their families have echoed these discourses as well. The viral video platform *TED* held one of its conferences in Galicia, Spain, in 2015. Cristina Palacios, president of ARELAS, an association of families of trans minors, shared these opening words:

When a baby is born, it's always the same. We look at the baby's genitals and if there's a weenie, a penis, it's a tough little guy, a boy. If there's a vulva, a vagina, it's a beautiful little girl. It's that simple. Today we know that transgenderism is a biological phenomenon, something innate. And that sex, in addition to the gonads, chromosomes, and genitals, is also in the brain. And the brain trumps all the other organs. That is to say, if your brain is male, you're a boy. A little boy with a vulva, yes, but a boy like any other. And the same thing happens in little girls. Little girls with penises, transgender girls. As the great sexologist Joserra Landa says, sex doesn't come from what we have between our legs, but from what we have between our ears.

The words do not surprise me; what surprises me is that they are presented as new and innovative. Trans activism's critical discourses were erased in one fell swoop as doctors, experts, and treatments step back into center stage. In the case of the Catalan show "Transit," it was frankly disappointing to learn that they had cut out all interviews with the trans teenagers who expressed a critical perspective on the medical model and gender binaryism. After the Joves Trans de Barcelona [Trans Youths of Barcelona] organization called them out for it on social media, the station, months later, aired a new version of the episode that included some of the interviews that had been previously edited out. I don't know if it was much of an improvement: they simply rebroadcast the entire documentary with the same people repeating the same medical discourses and just tacked on some dissident opinions at the end. It was obvious that the first edition had censured those voices because they questioned the predominant biological model and denounced the normativization of gender in our society.

With the emergence of "transgender minors" many of the doctors who had been previously undermined saw their chance to step back into the spotlight, offering solutions to the problems of trans people. It was also an opportunity for new social scientists to propose their own theories, but not precisely from a critical perspective. This is the case with some strands of sexology, which present themselves as having a more modern stance on transgenderism than psychiatry but which have not called into question the underlying hegemonic framework of gender essentialism. Depathologization, in my opinion, means we don't call it an illness anymore, yes, but it means more than that. It means understanding the trans issue beyond something biological that requires medical solutions and instead as something social, cultural, and political. When we started the movement for trans depathologization in Spain it seemed obvious to us that what we were proposing was a criticism of gender essentialism and that we had achieved our goal. We were wrong: the concept of depathologization has been reincarnated in new medicalizing discourses. A depathologizing proposal can still be profoundly medicalizing, essentialist, and innatist. Only from the innatist framework is it possible to think that a person can be transgender at age two, to think that gender identity is something biological and expressed at the most tender of ages and therefore something that can be treated starting at that age. Before, to be transgender was an illness, now it's a natural condition you are born with but, in the end, something biological and innate.

Just as with trans adults before, the medical model has a solution for being transgender in minors. Now they talk about hormonal blockers. What a surprise, another medical solution based in the modification of trans people's bodies. Let's go!

The Sooner the Better

I could almost say the whole reason I wanted to write this book was to be able to write the following paragraphs. I'm sincerely very concerned by the narrative on the body being furthered by movements in defense of transgender minors. It seems that the entire projection of these young people's futures is founded in the notion that their lives will be much better if they don't look like trans people and can pass unnoticed as adults. It is clear from the discourses of many support organizations for trans minors that they feel an urgent need to facilitate the changing of these children's bodies as soon as possible. And I think that this is a fairly problematic notion for several reasons.

First of all, I'm struck by the central importance given to hormonal blockers, as if this were the definitive solution to the problem, as if they were some antidote to transphobia. Treatment using hormonal blockers, which has been developed in recent years, consists of administering a medication to halt the development of puberty and therefore stop secondary sexual characteristics from developing. The treatment is maintained until the person can begin hormone therapy in order to masculinize or feminize their body according to their gender (Mujika and Mujika, 2014). The argument in favor of hormonal blockers focuses on anticipating a possible future problem. Hormonal blockers, the thinking goes, should be utilized just in case. Just in case the person wants to transition as an adult, so that they won't have to modify their body, a body with which they obviously won't identify. It is taken as a given that the trans journey must always, necessarily, include modification of the body. In practice, I have the sensation that once the process is started there's not much room for any doubt. Parents of transgender minors talk about hormonal blockers as if they were more like some kind of waiting room for the later hormonal treatments and surgeries than something preventative, just in case the person wants to modify their body later on in the context of a gender transition.

Secondly, I think it is very important that people who undergo gender transitions in childhood and adolescence develop certain tools to reinforce their self-esteem. These tools could include having a positive view of trans people, becoming active in the trans community, meeting other trans people, and having positive trans role models to look up to. This implies having role models that promote body positivity and acknowledge that the trans experience doesn't disappear after you change your body. Being trans is not an error that has to be corrected, or a scar that has to be erased. It's one way of experiencing gender among many others. And it doesn't disappear. No matter how much you modify the body, there will always be things that are different from a cis person's body: you will be a woman who won't have your period, who won't be able to get pregnant, or you will be a man who could get pregnant, who will never reach a certain height, you will have certain scars, etc.

On the other hand, when we insist on the importance of modifying the body as soon as possible, what we're basically saying about the bodies of visibly trans people is that they are not desirable, that it is better not to look like them. And that's not the best starting point because, first of all, these kids may end up being visibly trans anyway, and secondly, because the underlying idea is that it is better to pass unnoticed. Yes,

I understand that transphobia exists in our society. But the impact of transphobia is much more damaging to someone who has hidden their entire life at all costs from being singled out as trans than it is for someone who has reconciled with their difference. These young people need to hear that looking trans is fine and that there are many people who are noticeably trans who are very happy. Trans boys and girls should be able to imagine themselves as adults looking in the trans mirror and not in the cis mirror. Because they are trans. I tried to explain this idea in an interview for a print media outlet in 2015. A few days later I received an e-mail from the representative of an association of families of trans minors. In the message they expressed their discomfort with one of my responses in the interview. What I said was: "When a boy starts the transition to become a girl, it should be explained to them that they aren't going to become a woman, they'll become a trans woman. They won't be able to make every single male physical characteristic disappear." In their message, this person told me that when someone makes the social transition to be recognized as a girl, that person is a girl and not a boy and it's offensive to treat them as anything else.

I offered this response:

[...] The problem is that trans people (obviously generalizing) often look at ourselves in the "cis" mirror when we think about ourselves. We are severely lacking in visible trans role models (and by visible I also mean persons who don't have a normative level of passing that allows them to live life without being identified as trans). This mirror effect is very harmful because only very few trans people can pass unperceived in their gender, basically because not all bodies can transition from one gender to the other to the point of becoming invisible. That's why I think it's fundamental that we create positive trans role models so that our littlest ones have trans mirrors in which to see themselves reflected and they don't have to live their lives constantly frustrated over not being cis. Because being trans is also a possible destination, an inhabitable space. And the frustration of feeling that if you're not cis then you're a monster is really terrible for our self-esteem. We have to combat this idea and create a space where it is possible to be trans without being a monster. That's why I think it's important to explain to boys and girls that they are trans, that they are not going to be cis, and that there's nothing wrong with that because being trans also has a lot of wonderful things about it. [. . .]

It surprised me that when I said "When a boy starts the transition to become a girl, it should be explained to them that they aren't going to become a woman, they'll become a trans woman," the response I get is: "When we talk about someone who is going to make a social transition to be recognized as a girl, that person is a girl, they're not a boy, and it's offensive to me that you would treat them as anything else." Since when is saying that a person is a trans woman the same as calling them a boy?! Is it offensive to say that a person who has undergone a gender transition to female is a trans woman? Wow!

I think that the person who sent this e-mail misinterpreted my words and I probably could have expressed myself more clearly in the interview (although it doesn't seem to me that this is about explaining more clearly but about lack of wanting to understand). Obviously, trans people can identify as men, women, nothing, or everything. I'm certainly in no position to deny anyone whatever gender identity they identify with. What I was trying to say was that in our minds when we imagine a woman, we imagine a cis woman, and that's why I think tacking the term "trans" onto this female identity is extremely important. I'm not saying this is the way it should be, I'm just describing what often happens at this moment in time. I don't love that this is the way it is, but that's the way it is. When talking to a person who has been assigned male and wants to make a gender transition, we should tell them that when they grow up they will be a woman but we should underline the fact that they will not be like a cis woman. If we just leave it at "woman," that little person will almost certainly project the image of a cis woman. Basically because, as I said, when we say "woman," what we all think of is a woman who was born with female genitalia. Telling them they're not going to be a woman, they'll be a trans woman, is certainly risky because it's easy to misinterpret, as if you were denying this person's female identity. But what I'm saying is that the best way to support this person is by helping them create a realistic, responsible, empowering, and positive identity. Maybe I'm the one who should be offended by arguments that imply it's wrong to tell trans minors that they are going to be trans men and women. If there's nothing wrong with being trans, what's wrong with what I said in that interview?

The US researcher Jessica Ann Vooris published the essay "Trapped in the Wrong Body and Life Uncharted: Anticipation and Identity within Narratives of Parenting Transgender/ Gender Non-conforming Children" (2013). The essay, which I highly recommend, can be found in the anthology *Chasing Rainbows*. Vooris proposes utilizing anticipation as a way to think about the use of hormonal blockers. This theory was developed by Adams, Murphy, and Clarke (2009) to talk about families' need to anticipate their children's future illnesses in relation to vaccines. Taking this reflection as a starting point, Vooris points out the risks of using the logic of problem-solution to anticipate circumstances that have not yet occurred and that we can't accurately predict.

I don't necessarily object to the use of hormonal blockers in transgender minors. What I do object to is the narrative that offers this treatment as necessary, as the only way to support them. Once again, the suffering of trans people is resolved by altering the body, and that is the underlying idea that I think we need to challenge.

One clear piece of evidence that blockers are put forth as necessary is the fact that families are exposed to very harsh messages to convince them that this is the best course of action. An easy example can be found again in the episode "El sexo sentido," where Iván Mañero says:

> Today we have very powerful elements, substances, pharmaceuticals that allow us to block puberty. Because puberty in the end is nothing more than the brain activating a hormone that begins to flow through the blood and starts giving orders to generate our male or female hormones and from there development begins. So, the inhibitors, what they do is keep this hormone in the brain from doing its job. It's that simple. And we delay it until we know whether we want that hormone to do its job [. . .] These kids need hope. If they don't undergo this process, the index of suicide in these patients is very high. Much higher than in the rest of the population. Twenty or thirty times higher in these kids and teens than in the broader population.

After hearing that, what sane parent wouldn't want to start treatment with hormonal blockers for their kid? Suicide rates have become one of the main arguments used by the movements in defense of transgender minors to explain the urgent need for hormonal blockers. I don't think it's at all fair to put families in the position of having to decide anything with Damocles' sword hanging over their heads, as if not starting hormonal blockers will presumably make them complicit in a possible future suicide. Parents shouldn't be coerced with these kinds of threats: the decision is much more complex. Families need to be able to converse, express doubts, to think things over. But what's most concerning is that this argument is also absorbed by trans children and adolescents. What they hear is: if they don't let me go down this path I might kill myself, because I will be so miserable. I can't prove it with statistics but in my experience working with trans support groups, the risk of suicide does not dramatically diminish once medical treatment begins. Hatred of the body or the self often goes much deeper, beyond skin deep, beyond body parts. Changing the body is not a panacea, it doesn't cure all suffering, it doesn't give a person a new life. There are trans teens with a complete passing who still attempt suicide because they remain isolated and misunderstood. Because what good does it do to pass undetected if you still feel alone, strange, defeated, or depressed? The body may be the place that trans suffering is expressed, but it is not the source of trans suffering.

In the midst of this battle over how best to support trans minors, a trans teen in the Basque Country took their own life in February 2018. The media focused on bodily suffering as the main hypothesis for the suicide, with headlines such as "Trans Teen Commits Suicide on Threshold to Treatment" or "Trans Teen Loses the Battle Against Nature." I say that we have the responsibility to support trans teens by bolstering bodily acceptance and self-esteem, by strengthening their ability to combat everyday violence, by being openly critical of the binary gender system that excludes them. I do not think it is at all helpful to repeat a thousand times that not getting hormonal blockers could lead to suicide, because that creates a falsely idealized image of these treatments as life savers. We're ultimately causing these teens more suffering every time we state that modifying their bodies is the key to their survival. And, most of all, we are feeding the demand for these treatments.

The last element I'd like to analyze is how trans minors assimilate discourses on childhood transgenderism and narratives on the body and what kind of subjectivity this permits them. To contextualize this reflection I'm going to use three examples of real-life situations I've witnessed in recent years. The first example is a mother who told me she'd contacted an organization of parents of transgender minors because she thinks she has a trans daughter. The association advised her to show her child videos of an operation (a vaginoplasty) on YouTube so that they could see there was a way to solve their discomfort with their genitals.

The second example is of a woman who in the question portion after a talk I gave asked me how she might relieve the deep anguish her son feels because he doesn't know if he should freeze his eggs or not in case he wants to have kids later on, since hormonal treatments might limit his ability to reproduce. I asked her how old her child was and she told me he was seven.

The third example is also from a talk in which a mother explained that her eight-year-old daughter was very sad because she wanted to have a vaginoplasty but she still had to wait ten years. The woman said she was worried her child wouldn't make it to eighteen if she couldn't have the operation early.

And I ask myself: are we maybe overdoing it with the information we're giving these kids about body transformation? Are we possibly creating more frustration than anything else, given that many of these treatments can't be administered for many years? Are we idealizing the notion that changing the body will lead to total happiness? And yes, what I'm saying is that I don't know whether, at age six, seven, and eight, these kids should be watching videos of traumatic operations or worrying about what to do with their eggs. It doesn't seem healthy to me. And it shocks me to see that, at some conferences organized by associations of parents of transgender minors, they seat their children in the front row, no matter who's giving the talk: surgeons with diagrams of all possible surgeries, endocrinologists talking about the famous Tanner scale, and so on. Beyond the fact that I don't believe trans community spaces should focus solely on how and when to alter the body, if an association decides to focus on this, I'm not sure it's appropriate to do so in the presence of the young people they're trying to help.

What I'm trying to say is, I think that transgender children are exposed to a lot of information, sometimes too much. And, most of all, they are exposed to a very concrete type of narrative that pins very high hopes to the alteration of the body. Because of all this, I think that these boys and girls are also having their bodies stolen from them in the most shameless manner. They are being stripped of the chance to experience their bodies any other way and their minds are being flooded with possibilities that will either be a long time in coming or impossible to achieve.

And some of you might be thinking that these kids should have the right to choose, that if it's their desire to have treatment, they deserve to understand all the options available to them. But when you hear that if you don't do it you're at risk of committing suicide, when every conference talks nonstop about the best moment to start hormonal treatment, when you've been watching videos of surgeries since before you were even ten years old, that's not choosing. What choice is there, when we know that the need to alter the body is constructed socially. When a trans person has been socialized in a culture that associates each gender identity with a specific body, they will most likely want to have an operation.

Some trans activists have been saying this for years: if only all the time spent on medical solutions to being transgender could be dedicated to empowerment, visibility, and body positivity. This new generation of transgender kids could have the amazing opportunity to flip this discourse around, but once again the body thieves have set up shop and are doling out their solutions. As I said before, I felt the need to write this book mainly to denounce the shameless robbery of these children. There are ways of addressing suffering over gender during childhood that don't center on the body, or that at least position the body in a different way.

However, I'm not saying that if a boy comes and tells us that he is a girl we should ignore them or tell them they're wrong. Not at all. I think we should always validate a child's perception of their own gender. Denying their experience will only lead to frustration, sadness, and confusion. But, while we validate their experiences, I think that, at the same time, in parallel, we can nourish their minds with critical ideas. The problem is, if you believe that gender is in the brain, the support you will be able to offer will be very different to what's offered by a person who thinks of gender as a tangle of social relationships and constructions. The starting point, the mental framework from which you can offer support, the underlying values about gender, identity, and the body, that's the key. Winning the battle for the narrative is important precisely in order to introduce other arguments on how to ease this suffering. For example, if I think that gender is in the brain, when my son tells me he's a girl I will think: he must have a girl's brain, we should act now to make it as easy as possible to be a girl. That is to say, he's a girl and we didn't recognize it, he's always been a girl, but we didn't realize. And that means changing their legal documents and beginning preparations to modify their body to keep them from developing into a man in puberty. On the other hand, if I think that gender is a tangle of social relationships and meanings, therefore not an innate essence, I will maybe think other things. In this case, when a boy tells me that he's a girl, I might suppose that they are in some way learning that they identify more with girls than with boys. I might hypothesize as to why this is, but I won't automatically assume it's something definitive, so I will explain to them that if they are a girl that's fine and that if one day they stop being a girl, that's fine too. And in the meantime, I will continue to dialogue with them and ask them questions that will lead us to a better understanding of gender and its more complex norms, obviously in a way they can understand them. I will try to show them examples of boys who identify as girls but are still boys, boys that identify with femininity, boys and men who are extremely feminine but haven't changed their names because of it. As I said, I would never deny their gender identity, I would just try to broaden their range of possibilities with the objective of helping them make their choice as "freely" as possible. That is to say, I wouldn't rush out to legally change their name or tell them that what is happening is that they are trans, because that would introduce the myth of the wrong body and that is something that I wouldn't want to be premature about. If this little person tells me that they are trans I will listen to them and support them in discovering the most diverse and plural trans imaginary possible, but I won't be the person to place them in this category. That a boy says they're a girl doesn't necessarily imply to me that they want to undergo a gender transition. It implies that the category "boy" makes them uncomfortable, they don't like it, it makes their life more difficult. This doesn't tell us anything about the brain of the boy who feels like a girl, merely about the categories "boy" and "girl" and what they are associated with. The two models of support I've presented start out the same, by validating the feelings of this boy who feels like a girl, but they proceed in very different ways.

Finally, I'd say the most important thing is to create a space during childhood that minimizes outside gestures of normative gender identification and maximizes exploration, experimentation with different identities, and allows room for questions and doubts. That's what support means to me. But I recognize that supporting someone is profoundly complex, and many families are doing the best they can. That's why I feel it's important to be able to debate the hows, whens, and whys, precisely because it's very challenging and requires an open dialogue.

Instructions for How to Empty Out a Radical Proposal

And, of course, you might say: but if the message that these discourses further is so problematic, how has it managed to filter so deeply into our social consciousness? Well, because the narrative and its marketing are frankly very good.

One reason that this narrative is so successful is because it's very reassuring. What kind of person could possibly be against these families of trans children unless they are a dangerous ultraconservative transphobic? Also, these children's stories have been widely shared in the media. Testimonies on television are powerful, but the reality is that many trans activists have decided to stop participating in these types of testimonial programs because it has long been felt that they don't truly increase visibility of a political proposal but merely recount a life story and the opinions expressed are later discounted by a doctor. And if trans adult testimonies are a television success, the testimonies of children are much more so. Showing these young people on screens in every home has been one of the greatest successes of these organizations' communications campaigns. But it seems to me that this goes totally against their argument that these kids could change their minds at any time. How can they change their mind if they've already appeared in five hundred newspapers, magazines, reports, and documentaries saying that they are the first trans minor at their school or the first trans minor in their city to change their name on their healthcare insurance card. If they truly have time to decide, it doesn't make sense to plaster them on covers with headlines talking about transgender minors.

Secondly, the leading organizations of families of trans minors are great at lobbying, something unprecedented in the Spanish trans movement. Trans activists don't typically accumulate the same kind of social and economic capital that many of these families possess, nor as many contacts and professional networks. But, even if we did have access to the same resources, I don't think we would have developed the same tactics to make ourselves heard. Some of these organizations have sent their spokespersons to make the rounds to all of the television debate programs, the morning and afternoon shows alike. And they are always armed with a clear argument, a first-person testimony, and a scientific explanation of what is happening. They've convinced public television stations to produce documentaries with casts they've hand-picked themselves, presenting the stories of their children and their most trusted doctors. And they've won the favor of public opinion. These associations have also managed to influence political parties, who have presented their motions at city halls across Spain, and their proposals have been used as the basis for legislative texts. These groups of families have been responsible for the majority of local laws on trans issues. Because of all this, I think this movement has, in a way, colonized trans politics, pushing aside the critical trans activism that had been working toward other political goals. And we trans activists let ourselves be pushed aside because we didn't know how to react.

Thirdly, these movements have been very smart in utilizing or usurping slogans from radical trans activism to make their ideas go viral. The most popular include: "Long Live Gender Euphoria," "This Is Trans Resistance," or "No Body Is Wrong." The problem is that they have taken these phrases entirely out of context. These slogans were created by trans activism to say something else. Before, when we talked about trans resistance we were referring to resisting trans normativity, we proclaimed gender euphoria to challenge gender essentialism, and we debunked the myth of the wrong body to denounce the supremacy of corporal modification in gender transitions. But it doesn't matter: they've made the messages sound catchy and even radical.

Fourthly, I think they're lying. When they talk about trans visibility, gender euphoria, or that there are no wrong bodies, they always use trans children with a "perfect" passing, who look like regular everyday children that no one would ever suspect were trans. And that's a big lie because it generates a false idea of social acceptance. As a strategy for increasing sensitivity I'd say it's poor, because what I want is for society to let us look trans, not to applaud us only once not a trace of being trans remains. So the tactic of winning social acceptance by making people melt over these beautiful and perfect trans children feels like a lie to the many people who feel isolated. If you don't believe me, think how differently people would react to a photo of the character La Agrado in *All About My Mother*. Night and day. The traditional ways of being trans that some would try at all costs to leave in the past are absolutely current; they have simply been swept under the red carpet that we've rolled out to celebrate the trans revolution.

The clearest proof of this movement's effective communication strategy is that they have managed to convince us that Spain is a more open society now that we've accepted trans people.

Spain is Trans or the Fable of a Country Against a Bus

In January 2017, an organization called Chrysalis Euskal Herria [Basque Country Chrysalis] carried out a campaign that consisted of placing messages on the billboards of buses in the Basque Country and Navarra. The slogan read: "There are girls with penises and boys with vulvas. It's that simple." Curiously, the words trans or transgender did not appear. But let's recall that a member of a trans minors' support organization had already explained in an e-mail to me that they didn't like the term "trans," so this was in line with that position. Under the slogan, in smaller letters, they offered statistics about the trans suicide rates we discussed earlier.

A month later, and in response to this campaign, the ultra-Catholic organization Hazte Oír [Make Yourself Heard]

launched a crusade against what they called sexual indoctrination but has also been called gender ideology. They plastered
their own messages across a bus and drove it through several
cities. The text on the buses read: "Boys have penises. Girls
have vulvas. Don't kid yourself. If you were born male you're
male. If you were born female you still are."

And then everything blew up. Spokespersons for organizations of families of trans minors lit the fuse by saying that
these buses endangered their children. Doctors who worked
with the trans community echoed their words and soon the
entire country had turned on the evil actors of Hazte Oír (who
of course pulled off the cheapest publicity stunt in history). A
judge even ended up banning the bus from driving on roads.
The entirety of Spanish society was outraged by such blatant
transphobia and I spent several days in shock. I hadn't known
I lived in such a trans-friendly country. I honestly had no idea
that so many people were so concerned with the rights of trans
people, but it appeared to be the case. Luckily, the blood soon
returned to my brain and I started to analyze carefully what
was happening.

In the first place, I still don't understand why trans people
are the only people who should have been offended by the
message on the bus. It is a determinist, essentialist message
that promotes a profoundly rigid notion of gender. And that's
an attack on everyone, not just trans people. The idea that a
certain set of genitals should lock you into one gender identity
is something that affects us all.

Additionally, I don't see why it should be so horrifying that
kids might see this message on a bus driving past their school
(some families told the news stations that they'd rushed to
cover their children's eyes as the vehicle passed). Aren't kids
exposed daily to messages exactly like the one on that bus?
Pick up any health textbook and you'll see perfect naked bodies
and information on the natural development of girls and boys.
How is it that different from the message on the bus? Don't

kids, every Christmas, choose toys advertised on the basis of their genitals at birth? These kids know full well that it's not considered normal to feel like a boy if you were born with a vulva. We've taught them this! So the whole spectacle of people covering their kids' eyes seems totally melodramatic and above all overwhelmingly hypocritical.

But what really made me fall out of my chair was when I learned about the viral campaign to denounce the Hazte Oír bus. It was an image circulating on the web of a pink bus covered in the following slogan: "There are girls with penises and boys with vulvas. Who cares? Gender is in the brain, not in the genitals. We support trans kids." The equivalent of a team shooting the ball into their own net. All that collective hysteria, only to end up saying that gender is in the brain, that it's there from birth, blah, blah, blah . . . How is it possible to denounce an innatist campaign using another innatist argument? Gender isn't in the brain either, dammit! It is just as problematic to situate it in the genitals as in the brain. It's an essentialist, sexist paradigm. It's a battle between two equally prescriptivist notions. One that presents itself as ultraconservative, and the other as ultraprogressive. And, of course, the brains behind this response were none other than the organizations of parents of transgender minors who managed to make the denouncement of Hazte Oír a trending topic even among conservatives who were suddenly allies in the trans revolution.

And that's how Spanish society was able to pat itself on the back for being so advanced and open, a friend to trans people. Only that it's not true. The collective self-satisfaction expressed in those days still surprises me. People really thought that something had changed. I realized this as I left a meeting of families of LGBT persons and a father of a trans teen came and told me that the bus had helped to raise a lot of awareness on the issue. He told me that he was in a group chat with all the men of his family (cousins, uncles, brothers, etc.) and to give me some context he added: "You can imagine what that's like, sexist jokes, tasteless videos, you know . . .". And then he told me that when the thing with the bus happened he was very surprised that no one made a single joke, just the opposite. Proof that the bus incident had raised awareness. I told him that it didn't seem so clear to me, but what I'd really liked to have said is that his family members are still a bunch of sexist jerks and that the bus had not cured them of anything. What's more, it's just the opposite: if those people said nothing off-color about the bus it's because the bus and the response to it were not truly that transgressive; they did not threaten the status quo on gender issues, they were seen as being in line with established political correctness on the trans issue. That's why so many people were so openly angry over the bus, because it had been presented as the enemy to be vanquished and, after years watching documentaries about trans kids, we couldn't allow our society to put up with the abuse of those poor innocent children. It seemed to me that public opinion was being controlled by puppet masters who decided what was bad and what was good, and the good was swallowed without any thought or critical reflection.

No one bothered to notice that Hazte Oír decorated a new bus to skirt the judge's ban with a different slogan: "Do boys have penises? Do girls have vulvas?" And I said: wait, do they realize they just created a slogan that could have easily been coined by the most radical trans activism? These questions were profoundly transformational. We should have stolen the caravan to parade it past all the kids playing outside at recess. It's a shame that, in the wrong hands, it was put to the service of such an unfortunate cause.

It's All Fun and Games . . .

It has to be recognized that many groups of parents of transgender minors have an amazing talent for generating narratives.

It's often a narrative that I don't agree with, but inarguably powerful enough to make people think that they have a transformational proposal when in fact their arguments are the most essentialist in the entire history of our country's trans activism. But they must always stick to the script and remain on guard. Because once you know everyone is listening it's easy to get careless, to cross the line. That's what happened around Christmas of 2016, just before the Hazte Oír scandal, when the Chrysalis organization launched a viral video on social media asking people to donate money to their project in exchange for a symbolic gift. The protagonist of the video: Nacho Vidal, porn star and father of a trans child. The gift: a personalized pair of testicles.

(Do it, go to your computer and type into the YouTube search bar "Nacho Vidal No Hay Huevos," watch the video, it's only 1:57 long.)

For those of you who don't want to get off the couch, I'll transcribe it for you:

What is it that moves humanity forward? Intelligence, spirituality, technology, solidarity, karma, likes? No. What moves humanity forward, what led us to walk on the moon, what drives us to cure illnesses, what pushed us to challenge the impossible, can be solely and exclusively attributed to that moment when one person says to another: do you have the balls? When was the last time that you truly made a decision from your balls? Something like shaving your head or stating that the Earth is round when the whole damn planet and the Spanish Inquisition says it's flat. Or being the first woman to run a marathon even if it means putting up with cruel, sexist insults and attacks. Or raising your voice in a country where you could be burned alive for being black and saying "I have a dream." You don't have a dream, you have a huge pair of black balls. Or proudly declaring that you are a boy or a girl, no matter what you have between your legs. What a pair of admirable, extraordinary balls. Yes, sir. Life is about having the balls, gentlemen. About being yourself. About living the way you feel. This Christmas season you have the chance to make a very special gift and help fund Chrysalis, the association of families of transgender minors that fights for their identity to be recognized. Gift these personalized balls. These families have the balls we're so often lacking.

This campaign, which in terms of gaining publicity is excellent, is frankly horrific in addition to being sexist and in terrible taste when viewed from the perspective of supposedly transformational trans activism. It's almost as terrifying as it is pitiful. But it's real! It's not a dream. Nacho Vidal, a heterosexual alpha male mainstream porn star, is giving us lectures about what it takes to undergo a gender transition. And to do this he runs through a laundry list of meritocratic, individualistic, consumerist, and sexist clichés. I couldn't identify less with the model of visibility that this campaign proposes. Up to now I've never enunciated this question, but this video makes me feel obligated: why didn't feminist organizations challenge this campaign, which is such a blatant defense of the kind of hegemonic masculinity that always sparks so much ire? It is unacceptable to save yourself from discrimination by stepping on the heads of the people in the movement next to you. Of course it gives you a leg up as you climb, but it says a lot about your political commitment to combatting oppression beyond what directly affects you. I don't want to assume that this silence from feminism is out of fear of being labeled transphobic, but I suspect that has a lot to do with it. And the kind of critical trans activism that is willing to denounce these types of arguments within the trans movement is very small; we need more voices to counter these messages. HELP!

Part III

Toward a Critical Trans Corporal Ethic

6

Passing

Without a doubt, one of the things that has interested me most about this wave of trans visibility is where it positions trans bodies in relation to the myth of the wrong body. And I'm sorry to say I won't be the bearer of good news. The body occupies a central role in these narratives: the focus is no longer on the body as a hell we're trapped in but now on the successfully modified body as paradise.

In this chapter I will try to analyze some of the strategies for trans empowerment prevalent today. Of course the word "empowerment" is reviled, but nonetheless it does a good job at expressing the popular conception of helping people become sure of themselves, proud of their uniqueness, and not ashamed of who they are despite being part of a group that is stigmatized in our society.

With the rise of new trans discourses in our collective consciousness, new forms of trans empowerment have also emerged. These new discourses describe what it means to be an empowered trans person, what an empowered trans role model looks like and who is or is not worthy of social recognition. Yet one message has managed to cut through the noise to become the dominant narrative and it seems to measure trans empowerment by the extent to which the body is bent to a person's will in a transition that erases all traces of our trans journey and at the same time transforms us into desirable persons. I'd say that what is understood as trans empowerment is taking a dangerous turn, something we've already pointed out in earlier chapters.

The success of a gender transition, socially speaking, is determined by each person's ability to make their body match the gender they identify with. In trans slang, this is referred to as "passing." Because of its importance, it seems to me worth evaluating "passing" as the end goal of gender transitions. In the following paragraphs I will attempt to analyze this trans corporal norm with its hidden classism, meritocracy, impossible demands, and the exhibitionist trend it is creating.

Tailor-made Bodies

The category of "transsexual" first emerged in the mid 1950s. Over the many decades of medical treatments attempting to cure our "illness" we've witnessed a profound transformation in the collective consciousness about what it means to be trans. Specifically, the ideas surrounding the corporal modification of trans people have changed. To cite one example, let's use Pedro Almodovar's famous character in *All About My Mother*, La Agrado (for whom I have a special fondness). This character is a font of popular trans wisdom and a portrait of a past time. I say past because, today, trans adolescents are unlikely to identify at all with this character. She would seem frivolous, if not monstrous, and representative of a very stigmatized lifestyle.

In La Agrado's monologue, she says "Look at this body, tailor-made" as she launches into a description of all the surgeries she has undergone in her gender transition. She lists them off ironically, and the audience laughs with her from a distance, like someone witnessing a sordid spectacle, funny on stage, but never in their homes, their families, or among their friends. But, by the end of La Agrado's speech, it is understood that in telling the humorous story of her failures, she is also recounting her successes in the *conquest* of her body.

In La Agrado's time, the late 1990s, the modification of trans bodies was not uncommon, but it was still viewed with disdain and it was seen as truly heroic to actually go through with it. Nowadays, in the 2020s, corporal modification is expected of trans people. That is to say, trans people's right to have surgery is defended, celebrated, and applauded. We value and respect the trans person's ability to achieve the "tailor-made body" that they desire.

Society has learned that being a trans ally means supporting their battle against their bodies or for their identity, a fatal dichotomy. Anything else is labeled transphobic. If you were to say to a trans person "I hope you will be able to reconcile with your body during this process and you won't have to go into an operating room" you will be seen as a total jerk, right up there with the people who'd like to see us exterminated.

When I say that a transition is measured by the degree of passing achieved, what I mean is that the myth of the wrong body has infiltrated our social consciousness to such an extent that people who want to be supportive understand that they have to declare themselves in favor of you operating on yourself, the sooner the better, where do I sign, and so on. From there, the classic response when you tell a person that you're trans is: "Wow it turned out great!" followed by "You can't tell at all!" These people aren't cruel, their intentions are good, what they are saying is that they are happy you've been able to get rid of the parts of your body that bothered you so much.

Passing unnoticed as a trans person is very highly valued in society, and can even save a person from the wrath of transphobia in many situations. That's why I say that passing has become the trans ideal. It is associated with the values that La Agrado was expressing in her monologue (although at that time her audience didn't take her seriously): authenticity, courage, perseverance, success.

The majority of trans references presented as successful in this new wave of trans visibility are precisely the people who pass totally unnoticed as men or women. And, just the opposite, visibly trans people, like La Agrado, are seen as outdated models that the majority of trans people want to distance themselves from. Trans people don't like to look trans – call it interiorized transphobia, call it survival – and this discomfort exposes the weakness of passing as supposed trans empowerment. Passing, in fact, is the opposite of empowerment, it means having to eliminate all evidence that we've gone through a gender transition, that our bodies have a history different to those of cis persons, as if looking trans were the most horrible thing that could happen to us. I'm not criticizing people for wanting to pass unnoticed. I'm the first one to pray that I'll pass in many situations, but at the same time I realize that the situations where I'm most worried about passing are the ones where I feel most unsafe. I merely want to point out that it is problematic to understand passing as the trans ideal and the key to social acceptance. And at the same time I am hypothesizing that passing does the opposite of empowering us as trans people.

To give credit to La Agrado and all the proud trans women of the 1980s and 1990s, we have to admit that they had higher bodily self-esteem than the trans teens of today. They walked with their heads held high, well aware that everyone could tell they were trans women. The problem today is that no one wants to seem trans, no one wants a trans body because it's a burden, it's a huge challenge every time you want to do something that minimally exposes it.

The Trophy of Passing

If ten years ago we were struggling to promote other options beyond corporal modification, today we have even more work to do. Passing presents a challenge in that it's put forward as the only possible model of success and it's very hard to get around that. Just five minutes on YouTube will turn up thousands of trans people recording nonstop videos of their evolutions minute by minute like a gigantic reality show of their experience. Most common are videos of YouTubers telling us how their first month on hormones has been for them, their second month, their third, fourth, fifth, sixth, seventh, eighth month, and so on. There's one type of video that seems to me especially paradigmatic: the ten-second clips showing a trans person's evolution over the past ten years as they go through a dramatic physical change from woman to man or the other way around. Although we know that many years have passed between the first and last image, the speed of the visual narrative inserts in our minds a false notion about the metamorphosis of the trans body. It associates the trans experience with the easy, immediate, and successful transformation of the body. Easy and immediate because it only takes ten seconds to achieve it, and successful because the result is a person with exceptional passing who you would never, ever know was trans. That is to say, we are seeing an individualist and even neoliberal turn in gender transition in which the body becomes the object of consumption. These videos serve as a kind of trophy to be displayed on the internet, shared on Facebook, and praised with thousands of comments. But above all they create reference points. Many trans teens starting their transitions are inspired by these videos, expect to achieve the same results, and are attracted to the YouTuber's success, making them more likely to upload videos of their own transitions to the internet in hopes that people will congratulate them. It seems to me that this establishes an idea of success based in corporal modification. A fairly toxic notion of success, very different to what I understand as trans empowerment; it's an elitist and exclusive ideal, which not every trans person will be able to achieve because for starters not every trans person will be invisible as a trans person. It's also toxic because it promotes total self-absorption and obsession with the body's evolution without any solidarity, community, or critical reflection. Just me and my body, which I mold to my will.

This is what Lucas Platero defines as the trans spectacle in the prologue to the Spanish edition of *Normal Life*, by Dean Spade (2015). I'd go even further and say that it has become a fetish, for the world and above all for the trans community. More than a cult of the body, what has been established is a cult of the individual's ability to transform it.

This egocentric aspect of the trans experience has swept away the discourses that proposed a critical view of the gender pressures and beauty norms that standardize the bodies of trans people – what has been called transnormativity. In a society where articles entitled "Ten Trans Men You'd Never Know Were Born as Women" or videos such as "My Gender Transition in Ten Seconds" are shared a thousand times in under a minute, it is very hard to defend another type of possible trans body. Social media promotes passing as a one-way ticket to social success and total happiness, and it seems impossible to contradict these promises. Today, the robbery of the body is far from subtle, but it is much harder to denounce than it was a decade ago. Now trans people are no longer defending the modification of their bodies with shield and sword as a way to save their own lives, but as something that will lead them directly to success. And who could be against that?

What is being sold is a specific model of transition in which people who were profoundly miserable at the start go through the process to become totally happy and above all look like a man or woman from a magazine. The price of trans acceptance has been the assimilation of trans experiences into the dominant models of masculinity and femininity through epic tales of heroic people. Like an inspirational message on a Mr. Wonderful coffee mug that champions positivity and masks an ideology based in meritocracy and individualism. A quick internet search will turn up countless Ted Talks, YouTube videos, and interviews that repeat the same version of successful trans people over and over. What they are in fact promoting is passing as success, and I think that we have to declare war on passing as the recipe for trans success.

Self-Made Trans

This concept of the "self-made trans" is an invention of the trans activist Pol Galofre, who hits the nail on the head with respect to something very worrying that is being repeated in many trans narratives. It involves the individualist discourse that the trans person is self made, in a battle against harsh and unjust nature which they manage to bend to their will through a gender transition. These discourses imply that a person need only sufficiently exert themselves to be able to achieve this goal. That if you work hard enough for it there will be a happy life just around the corner, with an amazing body waiting for you.

But it's a lie. It's a fallacy based in the meritocratic and classist idea that trans people who make the effort can achieve it, that all they have to do is fight for it. But surgery can't change everything you want it to, the body can't change in every way you want it to. If you're a six-foot-tall trans woman with a deep voice, you could undergo three hundred vaginoplasties but people will still know you're a trans woman when you walk down the street, with everything that implies. Your ability to pass unnoticed as a trans person depends on your inherited anatomy, the age at which you initiate your transition, your health, and your willingness to endure certain treatments, but also the amount of money you have. Social, economic, and cultural capital play a crucial role in the ability to pass. And effectively, not passing is often linked to poverty and lack of resources. If we continue repeating the myth of the wrong body and idolizing those persons who modify their body to the point that they can pass unnoticed, where does that leave all the people who, even if they make a tremendous effort, will never pass unnoticed?

Passing Eats Bodies

In the short term it might feel like passing solves a lot of things, but in the long run it's not exactly our friend: passing is a lifelong process that must be constantly fed. And what does passing eat? Bodies! If the thieves of our bodies are manifested in any form it's through these ideas that suck our blood and devour our bodies.

In less than a year I was invited to two events of the kind you should be happy to attend because they are "good for the trans community." The first was *Beauty Cult*, a congress on LGBT beauty (for once the material centered 95% on trans people and 5% on LGB persons, even if it was for a cause that was so . . .). The second was Miss Trans International, a trans beauty pageant where trans women from all over the world compete for the crown (with tabloid television host Jorge Javier Vázquez at the helm). But what am I complaining about? In a single year I learned about two events that used the words trans and beauty in the same sentence. Unheard of! Even so, I decided not to attend either. I'm not against the promotion of trans beauty, but I am against promoting a trans beauty standard that requires going under the knife. I'm not interested in beauty that deepens social inequalities or fosters exclusive body norms. I think that beauty should be something for everyone.

When I say that passing devours our bodies, I'm referring to the fact that the myth of the wrong body opens the door to infinite modifications that go well beyond sexual characteristics. Trans people don't only want to change their gender: if they can, they also want to be beautiful and sexy. Obviously. But, as I've already established, we're a limitless market. If you tell a person they are stuck in the wrong body and they will have to have multiple surgeries to correct this problem, they will of course use these surgeries to become better versions of themselves. Many trans people don't simply aim to construct the body of a man or woman, but a handsome and attractive man or a beautiful and attractive woman. For example, at one time in the United States it was common practice for trans men to undergo mastectomies and while they were at it they had some liposuction and asked the surgeon to sculpt chiseled abs for them as well. (Am I a man with a six pack who was born trapped in a body covered in spare tires?)

I think pinning all our expectations for the future of the trans community to the transformation of our bodies will result in resounding failure. I think selling the lie that trans empowerment means uploading videos of fast-food transitions can only lead to disaster. If it would at least make us happier, we could consider it, but not even that is certain.

Of all the trans people in the world: there are so many who will never ever pass unnoticed, there aren't enough surgeries in the world to make that possible. It's not going to happen. But even worse is that there are many trans people who do pass unnoticed and still feel profoundly unhappy, insecure, or depressed, and the world tells them that they have no reason to feel that way since they've achieved their goal. Only a small portion of the trans people I've met have managed to balance passing and wellbeing. This is not a scientific fact, just a personal belief based on the hundreds of trans people I've encountered over the years. For a long time, the other trans people I met wanted to have every existing operation as quickly as possible, because they were tired of sticking out and being mistreated for it. Today, I still meet people with this desire, but less often, and what has suddenly emerged are people who pass fairly unnoticed but who are exhausted; they find it hard to make friends, they are terrified of sexual encounters, they feel anxious if they think someone might suspect they are trans, and so on. The discomfort that accumulates in a person's body can't be surgically removed.

We'd be ahead of the game if we could stand up for our bodies and defend them tooth and nail. Because waiting on the other side is not the correct body, the body that truly belongs to us, a body more worthy of being lived in. On the other side is only an abyss, where we will never know for certain when we have achieved the body we long for.

Corporal Ethic

The main problem we face is that it is very difficult to question these narratives because they sound so perfect. It's almost impossible to make other points of view heard because you can't compete with an inspirational coffee mug. Even so, I think that trans activism has to take that risk and dispute the hegemonic version of what trans pride means. We need to start talking about a trans corporal ethic, an ethic of corporal modification. I don't think I'm exaggerating when I say that, within twenty years, if not less, being trans will be a fully socially normalized experience. But the important thing will be how we've gotten there, what normative model of transition has been established in the collective consciousness, what kind of reference points trans people will have available to them in relation to their lives in general and to their bodies specifically. Right now we live in the era of "If you don't like your gender, transition; if you don't like your body, change it." This implies an ethic of bodily modification that I don't think I agree with. It's an ethic that reinforces tired gender norms, in which endlessly changing the body is desirable if it can help a person achieve happiness. But it is above all an ethic that does not hold rigid social structures in any way accountable for our unease. Maybe we should stop to consider defending the right to live in our own bodies, to think about ways the system itself could make instrumental use of this defense without feeling threatened. We may be nearing the era of unrestrained bodily modification, superstores stocked with medical treatments of all kinds to help us change our bodies, but that won't make us more free. The focus, in my opinion, should not be centered on the right to modify your body freely but first and foremost on the freedom to live in our own bodies without suffering or violence, without pressures to change it that break down our self-esteem.

So, before it's too late, I'd like to consider several questions. How far will we go to keep defending the notion that we will live better lives if we change our bodies? Up to what point are we going to promote hormonal treatments and surgeries as the solution to suffering? How long are we going to keep begging the medical establishment to invent new surgeries to alter our bodies and eliminate our complexes? When will we say enough is enough? When are we going to stop thinking that the solution lies in slicing open our bodies and sewing them back up? How much longer can we justify this plundering? Up to what point are we going to swallow the lie that surgery is the solution to the suffering, when in fact we know it's a structural problem caused by the rigidity of the gender system? I say up to here and up to now. When I look toward the future it is very clear to me that I don't want to live in a society in which people feel obliged to go under the knife to make their bodies match an arbitrary standard. My idea of utopia is something totally different. We might be late, but there's still time.

7

Reconciliation

Maybe the notion of *conquering* the wrong body is my own personal survival strategy and maybe it won't work for anyone else. Maybe my criticism of passing is out of line. But maybe not. Maybe it will prove useful to other people who are also feeling that they've been robbed. This last chapter is written with these people in mind. I for one believe that other forms of trans empowerment are possible; I'm convinced that it is possible to take back our bodies. Independently of whether a person decides to have surgery or not, to take hormones or not, anyone willing to try can *reconquer* their body. It's a way of thinking, a narrative, a mental state, a challenge, but, above all, a dialogue with one's self. All the questions that this book poses have the singular objective of bringing us closer to living happy lives.

In this last chapter, I would like to put forth a way of thinking about trans empowerment from another perspective that does not necessarily require a visit to the plastic surgeon. To do this, I will propose some tools for building body acceptance that are very different to the ones offered by medical discourses. This chapter also aims to jolt us out of the trans self-centeredness that characterizes us, so that we might be able to look around and see what we can learn from other persons or movements focused on *reconquering* the body.

Bodily Self-Esteem

This proposal is not meant to be exclusive to trans people. Self-esteem is a collective construction that requires an entire social structure to uphold it. If we truly want to start a debate on trans ethics and bodily self-esteem we have to understand that we are going to need to transform the minds of all people. But the good news is that, if we manage it, we will also be able to transform many trans people's need to change their bodies.

I'm going to use a very specific example that explains what I mean. If we were to take a snapshot of the current trans population in Spain, one factor related to the body stands out sharply: the issue of having had genital surgery or not. Throughout my life, the majority of trans men I've met have not had any operation to give their genitals a male appearance. What's more, the majority don't have any intention of having this operation. The large majority of the trans women I've met, on the other hand, have undergone genital surgeries or were waiting to have one. This is not a minor detail: there is an abysmal difference in the desire for genital surgery between trans men and trans women. Why is that? There are multiple hypotheses. The first is that the results expected from the surgical techniques involved in a phalloplasty (the construction of a penis in trans men) are less than satisfactory. A second theory is that it is much harder to hide male genitalia, considering the kinds of clothes typically worn by women, and it's much easier on the other hand to simulate a bulge with a prosthetic and a certain kind of trousers.

But the hypothesis that to me seems most relevant and the one I want to center this discussion on is a different one. To explain it, we must first clarify that, just like in the rest of society, a large portion of the trans population identify as heterosexual. Over the last decade, most trans men I've met have reported having had satisfactory sexual relationships with cis women. I'm not saying that there aren't some challenges, but the majority have felt desired as trans men in their relationships despite not having modified their genitalia. However, the majority of trans women I've met had very few positive sexual experiences with cis men before undergoing a vaginoplasty. In fact, most of the trans women who have told me about positive sexual relations with unmodified genitalia have been sex workers. The rest have indicated that they believe it to be very unlikely to find heterosexual men outside the context of sex work who want to have sexual relations with them and who are willing to publicly recognize any relationship if they haven't had genital surgery. So, it would appear that heterosexual men have a problem admitting to others or even to themselves that they have had sexual relations or felt desire toward a trans woman if that trans woman has male genitalia. This makes sense to me because these men are basically the same as the high-school boys who said to me "Sorry, teach, but that could never happen to me." They are the same men who can't even imagine a possible sexual desire toward someone who has genitalia similar to their own. I think that this desire does in fact exist, as proven daily by the number of hits for porn videos starring trans women or the numerous sexual services that trans women sex workers provide to men. I'd venture to say that in both examples a large portion of these clients are men who self-identify as heterosexuals and who express in these contexts a desire that they'd be hard pressed to communicate publicly.

So, getting to the point: is it just a coincidence that trans men, who seem to be able to have positive sexual experiences without genital surgery, feel less of a desire to have this surgery? Is it just a coincidence that trans women, in societies where heterosexual cis men won't desire them sexually (or more like, can't admit that they desire them) if they possess biologically male genitalia, feel the need to undergo surgery? To put it another way, the ability to accumulate positive experiences surrounding sexuality and their own genitalia enables trans men to imagine living with their genitals. That is to say, we believe that we will be desired, that someone will want to walk down the street holding our hands. I'm not saying it's easy, I'm saying it's possible. We may decide to have the operation anyway, but we know that sexuality is possible without modifying our genitalia. Trans women, on the other hand, and I'm thinking especially of teens, know full well that it is highly unlikely that a heterosexual male will "risk" maintaining a sexual relationship with them unless it is something secret, and sometimes not even then.

Without a doubt, there could be other explanations for the contrast between trans men and women's desires to undergo genital surgery, but this specific hypothesis seems especially relevant to me. And it follows logically that if heterosexual cis men were more open or flexible in their sexuality and didn't have so many homophobic ghosts haunting their minds, if they could truly be for trans women what heterosexual cis women are to trans men, if that were possible, trans women would have fewer gender surgeries, many of them wouldn't even want to have the operation, like so many trans men who have no desire to have phalloplasties. That is to say, that the need to modify the body is constructed symbolically and socially, based on the possible lives a person can imagine living in the body they inhabit, the environment in which they have to inhabit that body, and the range of sexual possibilities available to them in that body.

A few years ago, I heard the Argentine intersex activist Mauro Cabral say at a conference that the ultimate transformation will be when stigmatized bodies are incorporated into communities of desire. They explained that it was not about seeing a photography exhibition of trans or intersex persons on the walls at a party, but that the people at the party think that they'd love to go home with a trans or intersex person afterwards. The key lies in those bodies being eroticized (and not fetishized) and being allowed to exist in the sexual imaginary as something positive.

When a teenage trans girl asks me if I think a heterosexual cis boy from her class will want to become romantically involved with her if she hasn't had an operation, it is very hard for me to lie to her. The reality is that I think it's fairly unlikely to occur, even if these same boys consume trans porn or are clients of trans sex workers. In fact, I think she's more likely to explore her sexuality with other trans or cis women or even with trans boys than with a heterosexual cis boy.

All this is to say that, if we want to decrease trans women's discomfort with their bodies and their need to surgically modify their genitals, we have to work on the collective consciousness of heterosexual males, urgently. And I for one want that need to modify the body to be less dire because behind it there is suffering. A suffering I wouldn't wish on anyone. And I do think it's possible to live with much smaller measures of this suffering, but we are going to have to work a whole lot to get there.

The Other Wrong Bodies

In this section I'd like to make an uncomfortable yet necessary criticism of trans activism, and it is that we've constructed a debate that does not allow us to question why so many ideas are off limits. When someone says something that breaks the mold of what has been established as acceptable to say about trans issues, they are immediately labeled as transphobic. And that has created a kind of bubble of exceptionality around trans issues that prohibits us from thinking critically, prohibits us from thinking, period. And this is very dangerous. I'm aware that what bothers me about the trans debate is extending to all debates surrounding social "minorities" and that accusations of privilege or phobia are launched like projectiles at anyone with a differing opinion in order to discredit them. This creates a narrowmindedness and above all limits our critical thinking capabilities and leads us to become more dogmatic.

Part of this trend is closely linked to the identitarianism spreading through most social movements, or better yet, extending across our culture in general. I often ask cis persons if they think it's possible to be born trapped in the wrong body. Their unwillingness to respond speaks volumes. Then I state that I don't think it's possible, and suddenly the oxygen rushes back into the room. Many people suddenly say: "If you say it, then I can say it too," "I didn't dare to say it because I'm not trans," "I've thought it many times, but I've never said it out loud because I don't want to be misconstrued." It's a disaster: please, non-trans (cis) persons of the world, say what you really think, you sometimes have good ideas! Creating a bubble of exceptionality around transgendered individuals that makes most people prefer not to speak out critically on certain sacred postulates is the worst thing we can do for the trans movement. It's exactly through this lack of ability to question, this barricading ourselves behind limiting, falsely liberating discourses that we have had our bodies stolen from us.

I am sincerely concerned by the identitarianism emerging in the trans movements, something that many trans activists do not agree with; in fact, I come from a political tradition that has always organized in collaboration with cis persons, cis men and women in general and feminist lesbians and militant dykes specifically. I don't share the idea of silencing voices that could add to the trans debate simply because they come from cis persons. And this new form of essentialism is presented as transformational but it limits all possibility of articulation with other struggles. It promotes victimization, blocks all debate and exchange of opinions, and reifies the essential difference between the trans and cis experiences, something that I don't agree with at all. Being trans is not an essence, it is affected by many other social structures that determine the experience for each person. From the 1970s, when gays and transvestites first took to the streets in my city, to the trans collectives fighting for the right to legalize sex work, to the struggle for trans depathologization in the 2000s, in all these contexts the trans/ cis difference wasn't considered a threat to the trans movement. Today, it is.

Feminism, on the other hand, at the moment in Spain, is more open than ever to proposals from trans activism, and paradoxically trans activism is more hostile to feminism than ever. With the popularization of the concept "cis," there have been constant accusations of people speaking "from their place of cis privilege." I think that these categories should be used as tools to aid the movement and not as flamethrowers to incinerate arguments and exclude people from debates. That's not the kind of trans activism that interests me. But I will say that this thing happening in the trans movement is not something we invented ourselves; the movement is repeating dynamics learned from other struggles such as some strands of feminism and some anti-racist movements, among others. In any case, I'm in favor of trans activism remaining open to anyone who wants to combat gender binaryism, the rigid relationship between body and identity, trans essentialism, and so on. Anything else, in my opinion, is simply moving from one form of essentialism to another: the one that promotes sexualization of the brain to the one that proposes that only trans people can talk about trans issues. They seem like very different forms of essentialism, but there is in fact a lot of overlap. Neither the essentialist nor the identitarian discourses help combat the origin of transphobia and they don't exert any transformational or transversal force against gender violence.

Returning to the start of this section, I wanted to go beyond what is considered politically correct in the trans debate. The idea that I want to propose is that trans people have a significant privilege compared to other persons with stigmatized corporal experiences. The myth of the wrong body is itself a privilege; it's a theory that today functions as inarguable justification for the modification of our bodies. I say today because I recognize that it hasn't always been this way. What I mean is, if you are a trans person, it is understood that you have the right to change your body because it is the wrong body. However, for fat persons there's no wrong body narrative to turn to. They just have to deal with it. Here, I use the word "fat" based on the aesthetic canons imposed by our society, alternating between the terms "fat persons" and "persons who are fat" because I'm not sure which is the preferred nomenclature. The debate over fat as an identity or fat as a condition is a difficult one. Fatness is not an essence, but some fatphobia activists do propose that being fat is a political identity, among other things. In any case, I use these terms not to deepen the stigma but because I support the political resignification that these activists propose.

But first let's return to the myth of the wrong body as a privilege. It's a privilege because it legitimizes us when it comes time to demand that our bodies be modified and because it positions us as the victims of a problem we were born with that deserves immediate correction. It implies that being trans is something decided randomly by nature and that we've had the bad luck of being afflicted with. In contrast, a fat person is seen as impulsive, capricious, lazy, sedentary, or unable to go on a diet and get their butt to the closest gym. Something like "Well, they're perfectly capable!" Not like the poor trans people who have no control over their misfortune, who were simply born in the wrong body. That gives us the right to the restoration of our true bodies. The popular narrative on fat persons is problematic because it's judgmental and places blame; unlike the narrative on trans people, which is much more empathetic to our suffering. Which is why I say, having the myth of the wrong body to fall back on could even be seen as a privilege.

As much as I hate it, in the end this discourse protects us and legitimizes our demands to change our bodies. Surely there are many people with bodies that fall outside the standards of what is considered normal in our society who would like to be able to say they are trapped in the wrong body. And to have their suffering addressed without being blamed for it. If the objective is to have a body that is socially accepted, the myth of the wrong body is a privilege for trans people because it justifies our demands to change our bodies. But I'd say that this is not the objective. The objective comes before that: we don't need to have a body that is accepted by society, we need society to accept the diversity of human bodies. Although in the short term this myth might offer us a certain privilege, it's actually a trap.

Let's move on. I ask myself: why don't fat people have access to the narrative of the wrong body? Why don't we think of fatness in the same way as transgenderism and say that this is a skinny person trapped in the body of a fat person and so the public health system should ensure them access to treatment to modify their bodies? Or what would we think if a black person told us that in reality they were a white person born in the wrong body? These questions are absolutely cringeworthy, but I think it's a serious mistake not at least to consider what the answers might imply. I am not proposing that we transfer the myth of the wrong body to all bodies that suffer stigmatization. I just want to consider how we'd view the myth of the wrong body if it was applied to other corporal experiences such as fatness.

In our society people are blamed for being fat, which is a shame, but it at least grants these persons some agency over their own bodies. It is granted in a negative way, used to insult them, overestimating their true agency, to be sure. But an agency exists. And, in fact, many persons who are fat have empowering experiences of resisting the social stigma. Trans people aren't granted this same agency over our bodies, basically because it is understood that it's a problem we are born with, because there's been some short circuit somewhere along the way (see the shower of hormones in the mother's belly) that has made our bodies wrong. There's no agency to be had because the person has not chosen this body. They simply have to change it for a new one. And, because of this, we haven't been able to develop tools to reconcile ourselves with our bodies, to resist the social markers engraved in them. On the other hand, and without trying to idealize fatness, I think that persons who are fat have been able to develop many more strategies to build their self-esteem without having to undergo surgery. Conclusion: we have a lot to learn from fat persons. Truly, we could learn from their way of addressing their discomfort with their bodies and their ability to explore their sexuality despite the huge stigma placed on them. Fat persons are persons with a diverse range of body types that fall outside of what is socially accepted and who have empowered themselves through the development of a critical challenge to the pressures placed on them to change their bodies.

A few months ago I went to see a show in Can Batlló, an old factory in Barcelona that was taken back by the community. The show was put on by an activist group called Fat Cabaret. In it, a group of women gave performances, singing, dancing, or reciting monologues, either alone or in a group. The central theme of their performances was their relationship with their bodies and the stigma they experienced for being fat. Their words were profoundly painful and at the same time profoundly liberating. These women were in full-on process of *reconquering* their bodies. They made me feel a little stronger and a little less alone and without a doubt they confirmed in my mind that the body thieves could be outsmarted. I still haven't recovered from what I felt that afternoon. The spirit of their show was incredibly ground-breaking, but above all it was contagious. I hope they never stop telling their stories and continue to get on stage and sow their seeds of liberation in the audience.

There's one more anecdote I want to share. A little while ago I discovered a YouTuber named Soy una pringada [I'm a Loser] whose reflections on our society's hostility toward difference honestly warrants an entire book in itself. Among their videos, I'd like to analyze one in particular that made me think a lot about trans people. It's called *Carlota Corredera* [*Fat Traitor*]. To put it in context, Carlota Corredera is a talk show host and television director who has become famous for her work with La Fábrica de la Tele, an important TV production company that has created programs mainly for the Telecinco network such as *Sálvame* or *Cámbiame*. The problem is that Carlota Corredera, who in general works behind the scenes, recently explained that for her entire life she's been fat and that only recently was she able to stick to a diet and lose 130 pounds and that she's now much happier. (Here's the moment when you put down the book and go watch the video. It's 12 minutes and 24 seconds.)[1] So Soy una pringada makes a video criticizing her for talking about her life as a fat person like it was some hell because it is profoundly disempowering for people who are fat, who are trying to lose weight and can't or who experience frustration and suffering over their weight. That's why she calls her a "fat traitor" and insists that this betrayal lies not in having lost weight but in being ashamed of having been fat, denying her past. And I think: isn't it a little like the debate over passing but in the context of fatness? This video brought me back to the idea that the trans experience can't be thought of as vastly different to other forms of suffering related to the body. In the end, the concept of passing, which has emerged as the goal of gender transitions, can be reimagined as a way to politicize other types of stigmatization. For example, we can think of passing as compared to hiding

---

[1] "Carlota Corredera, Gorda Traicionera" by Soy una pringada https://www.youtube.com/watch?v=Qi4QH2PN508

the corporal modifications people undergo to hide the marks of cancer or HIV treatments.

Going back to the YouTube video, I agree with Soy una pringada that we can't deny our experiences, our bodies. We can decide to change them, but we don't need to feed the collective hatred of them. Or as Violette, a trans friend of mine would say, paraphrasing Soy una pringada: we can't let ourselves become trans traitors. We're not that different and we're not going through anything so different to what many other people go through. The more we close ourselves inside our bubble of exceptionality, the more we reject any alliance with other persons that live in stigmatized bodies, the further we will be from *reconquering* our own bodies.

A Window, a Seed

Saying that we need to outline a critical trans corporal ethic implies starting a conversation about other options besides the modification of the body. What I imagine are dialogues about the body's limits, giving up the idea of the dream body, how to deal with frustration, how to reconcile with the parts of our bodies that bother us so much, the pain of living in such a hostile society so judgmental of body diversity. We need to begin to talk about these things, but above all to stop judging individual decisions, to stop assuming that those who can't accept their bodies and end up modifying them have failed at something.

Sometimes, the task of promoting a different corporal trans ethic feels like trying to sweep the desert. It seems impossible. But I'm convinced that it's fundamental to helping us live better lives. Sometimes it feels like drawing a window on a brick wall. It might seem absurd to sketch a window that doesn't lead anywhere in the middle of a blank wall. It's just an imaginary window. But over time this window could serve as the blueprint for a way out.

When I started my transition I was still a teenager, a fairly difficult one I imagine. I beat my mother, father, and sister over the head with the word transgenderism at a time when we didn't have even a tiny sliver of the representation we have today. And they did the best they could, as they struggled to understand some of what I was going through, and finally tried to answer my questions with courage and generosity. Some of the things that they did took me a while to understand, one thing in particular, which I understood only fifteen years later. When I started my transition, my father told me many times that I didn't need to change my body, that it wasn't strictly necessary or obligatory. And at the time it made me angry because it seemed to me that he didn't get it at all, that it was actually the most necessary thing in the world because how could I live in the body of a woman, it was not an option. I felt very sad because I thought that if I changed my body I'd be letting him down, that he didn't understand that my life was at stake, that he was going against something I felt so deeply. And in the heat of those battles he always said to me: "I just want to be your counterweight, so that you know you can always change your mind, that you can always go back." I took his damned counterweight as an attack on my decisions, rooted in transphobia, as if he were trying to convince me that I was really a woman. And maybe there was something of that in it, but at the same time what his counterweight did was sketch an imaginary window on my wall. I hadn't understood any of what my father said. Nothing at all. He drew a window on a wall that no one looked at, in the dark, useless, ignored for a long time. I'd forgotten about his counterweight until a few years ago. That counterweight, that window on my wall, is now the spot that lights up my room. I've been able to reconsider everything I thought before, I've been freed from guilt over not knowing what to do with my body (when it seemed so obvious that I had to have surgery), I've been able to reconfigure my trans journey. I can consider, even for a second, that it's possible to take back my body again. And it's in part because one day someone told me they wanted to be my counterweight. A restricting counterweight at one time in my life became a liberation at another time. He wasn't against me, he wasn't against my transition: he was against me feeling that there was only one possible alternative. My small family tried to keep my body from being robbed well before I did, out of love, or instinct, or both. I suppose they eventually gave up the fight, but the seed had been sown.

Epilogue

I Remain Trapped in a Body but it's no Longer Wrong

In truth, this isn't an epilogue. It's a space of reconciliation. If this were a children's choose-your-own adventure I would have added to the end of each chapter a message that said something like "If the content of this book makes you feel angry, frustrated, sad, or it goes against everything you believe, jump to the end and read the Epilogue." But this isn't an interactive book, so I have to hope that you've kept reading to this point.

Yes, I think it's very likely that some people will be angered over the ideas in this book. I'm specifically referring to persons who are in conflict with their bodies, who would like to change their bodies, who truly feel that their bodies are a curse and they can't and don't want to live with them. People who feel that the very title of this book is violent because it proposes an alternative and painful path that implies returning to the *conquest* of their body. Some people might find this simple idea so terribly painful that it's unbearable. Some people need time, or to go through a long process, or even to modify their body before they can even begin to imagine that some things could have been *conquered* in a different way. I myself am all those people: *reconquering* my body was for me a long time a terribly painful idea that I could hardly stand. I had to change my body before I could even imagine that some things could have been *conquered* in a different way. But the most important thing I've learned on my journey is that it's never too late to *reconquer* your own body. It doesn't matter if we've taken hormones, if we've gone through surgeries, it is never too late to start thinking about our bodies in a different way.

At many points in this book it might seem like I'm saying all this because I've never felt the absolute desire to erase my body completely, that I couldn't leave the house in it, an urge toward self-harm or mutilation, panic at the thought of being naked, avoiding sexual encounters at any cost. It might seem like today, at least, I have a fantastic relationship with the parts of my body that remind me of my female biology. But none of that is true. All of these things still happen to me; I have to make an effort every day to overcome them. As I said in the beginning, writing this book forms part of an almost therapeutic process of learning to accept my body, it's a love letter that I've written to my body. But this book by no means intends to pass judgment on the many persons who, like me, have decided for a thousand different reasons to change their body in order to live a better life; that would be absurd. Almost everyone we see around us modifies their bodies to feel better about themselves, to greater or lesser degrees. No one needs to feel guilty about it. What I want is to get to the root of it, the reasons why we make these decisions, to look the myth of the wrong body in the eye and say: ENOUGH. Our bodies are fine, the problem is how certain parts of us are interpreted in our society, the meanings and connotations assigned to them. And due to this, unfortunately, many people might feel the need to alter themselves. We will most likely continue to feel this need for a long time. But I want to repeat: modifying your body because you're told you have to, because you're told it's wrong, is not the same as modifying your body because it's a choice you make to live a better life. If your body is wrong, there's nothing you can do except change it; if you want to live a better life, there's a possible dialogue, there are many paths, processes, and alternatives. They are painful, yes, but they are possible. And we won't have to go it alone.

This body that I inhabit has felt at times like a prison. I've fought it, I've defended myself from it as if it were attacking me. I've suffered greatly for having been born in it and it has made me feel wretched, alone, isolated. The people who love me have tried to protect it from harm, have tried to inspire me with their love for it and to help me see it differently. And even though, often, these gestures were not at all useful to me at the time, they sifted down into some part of my corporal memory. I have been awed by others who have volunteered to show me their scars, their tattoos, their marks. And I learned most from the people who dared to face and overcome the pain involved in not modifying their bodies. These people filled my darkness with doubts and uncertainties like small sparks that lit up a barely perceptible path. These people gave me the strength and encouragement I needed to reject the myth of the wrong body even though at first I hated them, just as I know some people will hate this book.

This book is written from a place of profound contradiction, by someone who doesn't experience their body as a party but as a battle. Who feels that they remain trapped in a body but one that is no longer wrong. A person trying to *reconquer* as many parts of themselves as they can, one step at a time. And I wanted to get all this down in writing, in case it might help someone else, lighting another small spark in the darkness. We're not crazy, we're not alone.

Bibliography

Adams, V., Murphy, M., and Clarke, A. (2009) "Anticipation: Techno-science, Life, Affect, Temporality," *Subjectivity*, 28 (1): 246–265.

Coll-Planas, G. (2010) *La voluntad y el deseo. La construcción social del género y la sexualidad: el caso de lesbianas, gays y trans*, Egales, Barcelona / Madrid.

Coll-Planas, G. (2012) *La carne y la metáfora. Una reflexión sobre el cuerpo en la teoría queer*, Egales, Barcelona / Madrid.

Coll-Planas, G., Alfama, E., and Cruells, M. (2013) "Se_nos gener@ mujeres. La construcción discursiva del pecho femenino en el ámbito médico," *Athenea Digital*, 13 (3): 121–135.

Fausto-Sterling, A. (2006) *Cuerpos sexuados*. Melusina, Barcelona. https://www.melusina.com/libro.php?idg=4614

Foucault, M. (1992) *The History of Sexuality. Volume 1, The Will to Knowledge; Volume 2, Use of Pleasure*, Penguin, London.

Meyerowitz, J. (2004) *How Sex Changed: A History of Transsexuality in the United States*, Harvard University Press, Cambridge.

Missé, M. (2013) *Transexualidades. Otras miradas posibles*, Egales, Barcelona / Madrid.

Mujika Flores, L. and Mujika Flores, I. (2014) *Los bloqueadores hormonales en púberes y adolescentes*, Aldarte, Bilbao.

Platero, R. L. (2015) "Prologue" to the Spanish Edition in D. Spade,

Normal Life: Administrative Violence, Critical Trans Politics, and the Limits of Law, Duke University Press, Durham.

Sales, A. and Tasias, I. (2012, 29 de agosto) Entrevista a Antonio Centeno: "Se nos reservan tres vías para alcanzar la dignidad: la de Ramón Sampedro, la de Superman y la de Stephen Hawking," Derechos Humanos ¡YA! goo.gl/PAFMxJ.

Serano, J. (2007) *"Skirt* Chasers: Why the Media Depicts the Trans Revolution in Lipstick and Heels," in *Whipping Girl: A Transsexual Woman on Sexism and the Scapegoating of Femininity*, Seal Press, Berkeley.

Spade, D. (2015) *Normal Life: Administrative Violence, Critical Trans Politics, and the Limits of Law*, Duke University Press, Durham.

Stryker, S. (2017) *Transgender History: The Roots of Today's Revolution*, Seal Press, Berkeley.

Vooris, J. A. (2013) "Trapped in the Wrong Body and Life Uncharted: Anticipation and Identity within Narratives of Parenting Transgender/Gender Non-conforming Children," in F. J. Green and M. Friedman (eds), *Chasing Rainbows: Exploring Gender Fluid Parenting Practices*, Demeter Press: Toronto.